From Preaching on the Streets To Pastoring in the Pulpit

With An Emphasis On Evangelism

by

Dr. Jayel Jacobs, Jr.

Unless otherwise indicated, all scripture quotations are taken from the King James Version of the Bible.

Verses marked LB are taken from the Living Bible

First Printing, September 1996

From Preaching On The Streets
To Pastoring In The Pulpit
With An Emphasis On Evangelism

Christian Life Missionary Baptist Church
4621 N.E. 23rd Street
Oklahoma City, Oklahoma 73121

Printed in the United States of America.

Published by Campbell Rd. Press
1129 Campbell Rd.
Oklahoma City, Oklahoma 73111

Library of Congress Catalog Card #95-74930
ISBN: 1-882581-113

DEDICATION

This book is

dedicated to

my wife, Joyce,

my children: Deya, Jayel III, and Joseph,

the Christian Life Missionary Baptist Church Family,

my parents, and other members of my family.

ACKNOWLEDGMENTS

I am truly grateful to all the outstanding Christian Life Members who have been a continued source of encouragement in completing this book.

To Mrs. Johnnie Stevenson, Bessie Ford, Mildred Pearson, Linda McClarty, and Vanessa Young, who graciously consented to read or type the manuscript, you were a tremendous help.

I am eternally grateful to my secretary, Mildred Daniel, who has spent countless hours typing and re-typing.

Thoughts from an old scrapbook

sent by

Lucy Sands

A dear supporter of Street Ministry Inc., 1979

****

You are writing a gospel,
a chapter each day,
by the deeds that you do,
by words that you say.
Men read what you write,
whether faithless or true——
Say! What is the gospel
according to you?

****

Contents

FOREWORD

You will be surprised that there are many Christians who do not know how to witness. They hear voices telling them that the Ministry of Evangelism is not important. Then they end up disobeying the voice of God and weakening the power of the church. To neglect the Ministry of Evangelism is the strategy of Satan. His plan is to keep men blind to the truth of the gospel. The world will be won to Christ through the Ministry of Evangelism. We need to understand the spiritual nature of evangelism. We live in a seductive world. Many of the things that surround us have been influenced by the New Age Movement.

Dr. Jacobs explains how Christ-centered evangelism makes the church effective in reaching the missionary mandate that God has given her. From the early stages of his life, Dr. Jacobs informs the reader that he was destined to do the work of God through the Ministry of Evangelism. I appreciate Dr. Jacobs' sound biblical approach to evangelism. Dr. Jacobs' insight, experience, and personal antidotes provide authenticity and a dynamic approach to evangelism.

The author seeks to understand the dimension of evangelism. He believes the best way for pastors to train their people how to witness is to biblically follow this important work and to educate the church on how to rely upon God's power and direction for evangelism. I strongly recommend that the reader read this book with diligence for its contents will yield much fruit in the days to come.

Dr. Cliet Wilburn
Christian Education Director

Street Ministry Headquarters and Study House

Christian Life Missionary Baptist Church 1980 - 1985

Present Christian Life Missionary Baptist Church

Introduction

While preaching on thirteenth and Walnut in Oklahoma City, Oklahoma, a middle-aged man came, listened, and heard the message of Jesus Christ from God. Being brought under conviction, by the Spirit of God, he took a bottle of liquor from his pocket, broke it, believed, and received the Lord Jesus Christ. I later had the opportunity to lead his family to Christ.

A preacher proclaiming the good news of Jesus Christ on a street corner compares with a fisherman casting his rod in a lake. Street preaching provides vast opportunities for reaching an individual, just as fishing provides opportunities to catch a fish.

Fishing is one of the most popular forms of recreation. People of all ages enjoy fishing in streams, rivers, lakes, bays, and oceans for many kinds of fish. Some people fish with simple cane poles, but others use rods, reels, and additional equipments that require more skills to operate. People who choose fishing as a sport are anglers.

Evangelism also requires witnessing skills and preparation. People who are fishermen for Christ are Soul Winners. They enjoy winning souls, by the Lord Jesus Christ. In **Matthew 4:18-19** we find these words, **"And Jesus walking by the sea of Galilee, saw two brethren, Simon called Peter, and Andrew his brother, casting a net into the sea: for they were fishers. And he saith**

unto them, Follow me, and I will make you fishers of men."

Various kinds of fish differ so greatly in shape, color, and size that it is hard to believe they all belong to the same group. Some fish look like lumpy rocks and others look like wiggle worms. Some fish are nearly flat as a pancake and others can blow themselves up like a balloon. Fish have all the colors of the rainbow, just as men are different colors. Christ Jesus is deeply concerned for all people everywhere. He created us for His purpose.

The Lord Jesus is concerned about people with various social and moralistic problems. He is concerned about people churched, unchurched, saved, unsaved, committed, uncommitted, and people that are reachable and unreachable. This is so important to the Lord that He compels us to proclaim the gospel into the hearts of men, women, boys, and girls.

People, like fish live in all kinds of situations. Fish live almost anywhere you find water. They are found in the near freezing water of the arctic and in the streaming waters of the tropical jungles. They live in roaming mountain streams and in quiet underground rivers. Some fish make long journeys across the ocean. Others spend most of their life buried in sand, on the bottom of the ocean. Fish usually do not leave the water. Some survive for months in dried up river beds, just as some people live in the metropolis, others in the suburbs, and even rural areas trying to survive without the Lord Jesus Christ.

God through Jesus Christ has commanded the Church, the Light, the Salt of the World, to evangelize humanity. According to the words of **Matthew 28:19**, Jesus Himself commands, the only organization and organism, to **"Go ye therefore, and teach all nations, baptizing them in the name of the Father, and of the Son, and of the Holy Ghost."**

The NAACP, Urban League, Community Action Program, Neighbor for Neighbor, United Way, and many other worthy organizations are doing great things for humanity, but they do not have the mandate to evangelize. If not the Church of the Living God, the Church of Christ, the Believers, the Called out Ones, then, who will? The church receives help in counseling, feeding, clothing, and educating people, but does not and will not receive help in evangelizing the world for Jesus Christ. If not the Church, which is the Body of Christ, and the Temple of the Holy Spirit, the Family of God, neither male nor female, bond nor free, Jew nor Gentile, then, who will?

The Lord Jesus Christ has given the church the power to witness with effectiveness according to **Acts 1:8, "But ye shall receive power, after that the Holy Ghost is come upon you: and ye shall be witnesses unto me both in Jerusalem, and in all Judea, and in Samaria, and unto the uttermost part of the earth."** Our mandate begins with our city, then extends to our state and surrounding states and into all parts of the world.

It takes many techniques to catch a fish, and various methods when it comes to evangelizing. To be a successful evangelist, missionary, soul-winner, or fisherman, many different methods such as: cast fishing (Street Preaching), still fishing (Crusades), drift fishing (Visitation), trout fishing (Door-to-Door), and ice fishing (Bus Ministry) could be of use. Whichever method you choose to use to evangelize will be between you and the Lord. I believe that evangelism is communicating the good news of Jesus Christ to the lost and not just the saved.

Not only are we compelled to catch men, but also commanded to make disciples. One responsibility of a pastor-teacher is to equip the saints of God to do the work of the ministry.

After four and a half years of full-time Evangelistic Ministry, the Lord led me into a Pastoral and Equipping Ministry. This book shares some of my life experiences, which explain how the Lord ordered my footsteps, to evangelize and disciple God's new people.

At the beginning of my evangelistic journey, while attending an institute at Bishop College in 1974, a Minister challenged me. He raised the question, "After you pull the fish out of water, what do you do with the fish?" To me, he highly suggested that leading a person to Christ was sinful without discipleship. I did not have the answer.

I remember crying and praying from Dallas to Oklahoma City for God to equip me to evangelize. As God began to teach me, I learned that the Holy Spirit was in partnership with every conversion. He has gifted some preachers to be evangelists, pastor-teachers, or some teachers. Some water, some sow, but it is God that gives the increase. Some witness a person being born again, and others witness his Christian growth as he becomes what God wants him to be. It is all part of evangelism.

In this book, the emphasis is on Evangelism. It gives some suggestions on ways that a pastor and church might evangelize effectively. Sharing some of my life experiences can best explain the success of evangelism in my life and ministry. These experiences have led me from **preaching on the streets as an Evangelist, to preaching in the pulpit as a Pastor.**

Evangelist / Pastor Jayel Jacobs Jr. becoming a fisher of men.

Evangelist Jacobs preaching in an apartment complex on top of his orange Vega in Jackson, Mississippi where over 70 people accepted Christ.

Chapter One
Evangelism Begins With God

While in Jackson, Mississippi, after about one hour and a half of preaching alone on the street, two police officers suddenly approached me demanding that I put up my microphone. I asked whether anyone had called complaining about my preaching, and they told me no.

The officers explained that I did not have a permit to use a microphone on the street. I readily agreed to stop using it and moved to an apartment complex, where a double homicide had occurred about thirty minutes before my arrival.

God led me to get on top of my 1974 orange Vega station wagon and begin to proclaim the good news of the Lord Jesus Christ as Savior and Lord. This was one of the most memorable times in my evangelistic endeavors, and it was the beginning of my evangelistic tours.

God Creates Us

Beginnings are powerful and they hold great significance in our lives. My own life originated with God through two astonishing parents, who had a solid foundation in the Lord Jesus Christ.

My father, Jayel Jacobs, Sr., and my mother, Opal D. Jacobs loved God and they were willing to obey the plan of God for their lives. Their marriage was blessed with the births of nine children: Eva Lois, Ruth, Bobby Joe, Walter C., Centel, Bethel June, Lavanna, Loretta, and me, Jayel Jacobs, Jr., whom they knew as "Son".

Above is a picture of the Jacobs' Family with the exception of my sister Ruth.

As stated in Jeremiah 1:5, "Before I formed thee in the belly I knew thee; and before thou camest forth out of the womb I sanctified thee, and I ordained thee a prophet unto the nations."

Also, according to Romans 8:29, We see, "For whom he did foreknow, he also did predestinate to be conformed to the image of his Son, that he might be the firstborn among many brethren."

Being the first son and third child of nine children, my life was truly predestined. My father's desire as a young man was to have a son. He tells me on July 16, 1946, it was a cool, bright morning and the wind was coming from the south. It was in a small country town, by the name of Goodnight, Oklahoma, where I was born. Little did I know, that even in my mother's womb, God was preparing me for a great work. In fact, all of God's work is great. He was preparing me as a mouthpiece, who would one day lead and educate others about evangelism and the Word of God.

My mother told me of an incident when I was two years old. She placed a wallet, a Bible, and an agriculture book on the floor in front of me and allowed me to choose one of them. I immediately chose the Bible and she said, deep within, she always knew that I would be a preacher one day. I am glad, even now, that I chose the Bible. My desire is that everyone would choose God and His Word.

Preparing for the work

As an adolescent, I was attempting to get others to go to church. My parent's commitment helped me to get a good Christian foundation and formed the basis for my spiritual growth. Often, my mother taught me Bible stories and explained Bible verses to me. The lessons my father taught me were the importance of work, and to be responsible for my debt and actions. Both were faithful members of the Church of the Living God, the Pillar and the Ground of the Truth. My father served as a deacon for many years, after which he accepted his call to the Gospel Proclaiming Ministry. Mother served as an usher and deaconess for many years.

God Saves

Mankind's greatest privilege is to become a son of the Living God. God saved me at the age of twelve, during a revival service at the Church of the Living God the Pillar and the Ground of the Truth where Bishop Herbert Dickerson became my first pastor.

Elder A. Long served as the Evangelist during that week. After attending the revival meeting, for five consecutive nights, God drew me, from sitting on the back pew Monday night, to eventually sitting on the front pew, by Friday night. That night, I gave myself to the Lord Jesus Christ.

I believe every church needs to be involved in revival meetings. The saved community should always remember to bring the lost to this kind of function. We, as believers, should begin with our immediate family, relatives, friends, employers, and co-workers. Throughout the Bible, we witness relationships coming to the Lord.

Revival meetings can be an effective way of reaching people, only if the church remembers the lost and unchurched. Little did I know how significant a revival meeting was in preparing me for an evangelistic ministry of the future. God was busy designing my purpose in life.

From my experiences, we can also learn that salvation is a process with a due time. We must sow seeds and give time for the seeds to bring forth fruitfulness through the working power of the Spirit of Christ. Often, we try to press individuals for a premature decision and that is just what we get. We need to work with the Holy Spirit and not for Him, whether inside or outside the church. Unnecessary pressure, for a decision, has stagnated the growth of many churches and the Body of Christ. I was given time to make a genuine commitment to the Lord Jesus Christ and the church.

Later in life, I received assurance of my salvation. This changed my life, and opened the way for me truly to evangelize. I could validate scripturally what I already believed was true according to **Romans 5:6, "For when we were yet without strength, in due time Christ died for the ungodly,"** and that God raised Him from the dead for my justification and **"For whosoever shall call upon the name of the Lord shall be saved."** They later baptized me in Washington's pond, which belonged to a family in our community. About twelve years later, Uncle Lo, Uncle Boone, and I used this pond to baptize more than 20 new converts. These converts had come to the Lord Jesus Christ, through a "Youth for Christ" movement.

God Does the Calling

As my parents took me to church, I began to grow closer to God and His Word. My first call was evangelistic in nature, in a dream, at the age of thirteen. The Lord appeared unto me and commanded me to **"Go into all the world, and preach the gospel to every creature."** I believe every man/woman of God should have a personal call from God. Our call is the foundation of our ministry and purpose. Without a call from God, there is no God sent person or ministry. He chooses whom He sends. My first subject and text was one in the same. The message was found in **Romans 10:13, "For whosoever shall call upon the name of the Lord shall be saved."** I wondered why most preacher's testimony was, "I did not want to preach", or "I ran from preaching." As a youth, I decided I would preach, if the Lord called. However, just like many others, when He did call, I ran. Nevertheless, the call of God was upon my life and he undoubtedly called me to preach. On the other hand, I did not surrender to preach until the age of twenty-three. Many precious believers waste valuable time placing God on the back burner until they feel the time is right for them to obey God. It is wise to say, "Yes Lord," when God calls one into the ministry. You need to know that God's call is always accompanied with God's help. A look at **Luke 4:18** should be helpful. **"The Spirit of the Lord is upon me, because he hath anointed me to preach the gospel to the poor; he hath sent me to heal the brokenhearted, to preach deliverance to the captives, and recovering of sight to the blind, to set at liberty them that are bruised,"**

I did not obey the voice of God then, because of the fear of failure. I realize now that we can never defeat God's plan or purpose because of His voluminous power to bring the good from every situation. According to **Romans 8:28**, All things not only are worked out by God for the good, but all have a purpose for happening through His sovereign will. So, rather than becoming a preacher, I became a Sunday School Superintendent at the age of fourteen. I believe becoming a Sunday School Superintendent at an early age produced in me a strong drive and vitality for total involvement of the entire church. I know now that a mentality existed back in those days that Sunday School was for children and not adults. This stronghold continues in many of our churches today. I believe, however, if the Sunday School grows, then the church grows.

As a Pastor, I have served as a Sunday School Teacher from the onset of the Christian Life Missionary Baptist

Church. My first teaching assignment was the New Member's Class, then, I formed an Adult Class or Pastor's Class where I was teaching both new and older members. Teaching new converts and older converts is very important. It is God's will for all of His people to become mature, productive saints. It is sad to say, but there are too many gray-headed babies in the church today.

It is a privilege to be hand-picked by Almighty God to work with Him in the vineyard, reconciling the world to Himself. Many pastors, teachers, evangelists, and missionaries will confess today that they struggled with the call of God upon their lives. When in doubt, pray. When doubt seems to linger, concerning a call from God, then volunteer. There are two ways to become a soldier that is to be drafted or to volunteer.

If one truly struggles with the call of God, then go ahead and volunteer. Remember Isaiah, who said, "Here am I Lord, send me," because disobedience to God is a "horrifying sin".

There are no accidents in God

Yes, beginnings are significant. Being raised in a small community and attending a rural school in Parker Heights by the name of Dunjee, my life began to take form. I thank God I had some strong authoritative teachers and principals, who were not afraid to discipline, not afraid to pray, and not afraid to bring God into the classrooms. These teachers believed in the Scripture, **"Train up a child in the way he should go: and when he is old, he will not depart from it."**

I remember vividly my 3rd grade teacher, Mrs. Moon, who took time to encourage me and Mrs. Hicks, my 4th grade teacher who pushed me to do better. Remembering my 5th grade teacher is easy for me. Mrs. Vickers, a Pastor's wife, taught us to recite portions of the Beatitudes every morning. Most important, the fifth grade is where I met my wife, Joyce. Other influential teachers were Mrs. Vertie B. Anderson, Rev. J.L. Trotter, and Mrs. L.A. Joseph, my home-room teacher, and my english teacher, who constantly declared to us to be all we could be. She also taught us that a good education was essential for a good start in life.

Mrs. Clara Luper taught history and made it seem real and very easy to understand. During the 1960s, Mrs. Luper led many of us in the Civil Rights Movement. Her work, and the work of others will have eternal dividends.

We had unique principals who were good role models such as Mr. Thompkins, Mr. Watkins, Mr. Factory, and Vice-Principal, Mr. Fowler. Rev. Parker was my agriculture teacher and sponsored the Future Farmers of America. I am thankful for the privilege to have served as president of this organization. Rev. Parker was always making a difference in the community. Little did I know, that he would become my Pastor at the Loving St. James Baptist Church. I remember Mrs. Doris Combs sponsoring the newspaper and allowing me to be the business manager. My first opportunity to act was in the english class of Mrs. Johnnie Stevenson, where I would have starred in the play, "Rebel Without A Cause", if it had taken place.

Today, I am a Pastor with a cause. That cause is evangelizing at home and throughout the world. During my high school days, we had many male teachers. Back then, many men took their rightful place as leaders. Among those who influenced me were: Mr. Oliver, a science teacher, Mr. Lurks, an auto mechanics teacher, and Mr. Ewery, another science teacher. It was Mr. Ewery who remarked, as I ran to the high school building to turn in my graduation robe, "Wear another one." I heard God, and by his help, I have worn three more.

I learned about leadership through football and my coaches Mr. Jayel Jacobs, Sr., Mr. George Clark, Mr. Robert Adams, Mr. Maurice Jones, Mr. Maurice Luster, and Mr. Alexander Jones. When I was in the eighth grade, Mr. Alexander Jones put me in front of Clarence Stewart, another player, who weighed more than two hundred pounds. I weighed about one hundred and twenty pounds. I hit him with all I had and the coach allowed me to play quarterback from this impressionable encounter. He saw I was not afraid, and I would not back down regardless of the size of another player.

That determination has also proven to have an impact on my life and my work in evangelism. I cannot say that I have not wanted to back down in some situations. However, the Lord gave me strength to conquer the many obstacles that I encountered. It reminds me of **Philippians 4:13, "I can do all things through Christ which strengtheneth me."**

I was quarterback my freshman year, linebacker my sophomore year, halfback my junior year, and quarterback and defensive halfback during my senior year. We were the first conference champions in junior high school, and the first high school conference champions in the history of Dunjee School. To God be the glory for all of His wonderful promises and all of my precious teammates.

Dunjee Grade School above and High School below

I did not realize it then, but this was the beginning of many situations where I would be the first. The Lord allowed me to be the first successful black sales representative for Kraft Foods, Inc. in Oklahoma City.

I was the first 1964 Dunjee graduate to graduate from college, and the first black Mountain Patrol Officer for the Juvenile Justice System in Denver, Colorado. Standard Life Insurance employed me as its first black salesperson. I was the first full-time Black Baptist Evangelist in Oklahoma and the first to organize an African American Church in Del City.

The Lord God permitted all these events in my life. He knows our heart, and sometimes, we are rewarded with our desires. On the other hand, sometimes God says no to our desires. My greatest desire in high school was to attend Philander Smith College in Little Rock, Arkansas. I had dreams of getting a football scholarship and playing football, and maybe "making the big times." Nevertheless, as God would have it, most of my teammates received scholarships, except me. I was crushed, and I could not understand it. Now, I know why. We need never forget, "Nothing bad can happen, to a believer, in the Lord," For God is in complete control. This scripture describes how I felt and what God was saying to me. **"...Weeping may go on all night, but in the morning there is joy." Psalms 30:5 LB.**

By the help of the Lord, I graduated the most outstanding senior male in high school. Then, I had to decide to go to the Marines or follow my girlfriend, Joyce, to Langston University, to watch her. I received a scholarship from Dr. William Hale, President of the University. So, off I went to Langston University on a $400.00 a year scholarship and $5.00 a month allowance from my parents.

Let me deviate from the narrative and tell some historical experiences I had at Langston. I did not know that Langston University would be the most difficult place for me to preach later in my life. Although I only spent my freshman year there, I had no invitation to speak on campus after being called to preach. It was God, who led me back to Langston University. Preaching in front of the student union around noon, from my car microphone was a humbling and challenging experience.

Due to my obedience to the Father in this difficult situation, the Lord opened doors for me to preach revivals, serve on symposiums, and other evangelistic engagements on the campus. A great revival also took place in Langston, Oklahoma at the New Hope Baptist Church, under the leadership of Rev. J.D. Ford, where more than eighty students were saved. Some of those students became part of the Street Ministry. Many became members of various churches, and others became members of the Christian Life Missionary Baptist Church. Some became preachers of the Gospel of Grace throughout the United States. Now, let us go back to the main account.

After a year at Langston, in my college days, I transferred to Central State College in Edmond, Oklahoma. This was a culture shock for me. I had attended an all black high school, and an almost all black university, and there I was, in a nearly all white college. What a wake up call I had. Nevertheless, I received a Bachelor of Arts Degree in Sociology with a minor in Psychology.

I see where God was controlling my path. He kept me out of situations that could have changed the course of my life. He led me into situations which changed my life and for which I am truly grateful. An example was my marriage to my childhood love, Joyce, who is a blessing in our ministry.

Jesus Christ, God's Ultimate One

The Lord has a way of positioning us for the fulfillment of our purpose and call. It states in **Genesis 12:1-3 "Now the LORD had said unto Abram, Get thee out of thy country, and from thy kindred, and from thy father's house, unto a land that I will show thee: And I will make of thee a great nation, and I will bless thee, and make thy name great; and thou shalt be a blessing: And I will bless them that bless thee, and curse him that curseth thee: and in thee shall all families of the earth be blessed."**

Abram had to leave his homeland in order for God to use him, and deal with him in the manner purposed for his life. My calling was and would be evangelistic in nature. Therefore, God had to teach me some valuable lessons before I could be used, according to His will. These experiences led to a spiritual awakening, which enabled me to realize God's purpose and plan for my existence. I too had to leave my homeland.

After graduating from Central State College in Edmond, Oklahoma, I had to decide where we would live. It was a difficult decision to leave my family. My father was very apprehensive about my leaving Oklahoma. God's road map led me to Denver, Colorado. I hitchhiked from Oklahoma to Hutchinson, Kansas with Mr. Curtis Webber. I traveled the remainder of the way by bus and arrived on a Sunday. I found myself in Denver, with a little more than $28.00 in my pocket, a few changes of clothes, and knowing no one, but God in the entire city.

My reason for going there, I thought, was to find a good job and seek a fortune. On the next day, Monday, God gave me a position as a Mountain Park Supervisor dealing with juvenile delinquents in a camp on Mt. Evans. They gave me a room at the juvenile center and I was allowed to eat from the cafeteria. God graciously provided for me according to **Philippians 4:19, "But my God shall supply all your need according to his riches in glory by Christ Jesus."**

My God truly made a way to meet my needs. Not only were my needs met, but He gave me some of my wants. Just sixteen days following my arrival, I purchased a new 1968, 440 Magnum, 375 horses, automatic, tomato red, black vinyl top, RT Dodge Coronet. After purchasing my new car in Littleton, Colorado, I started back to Oklahoma, in particular, to "New Chance City," near Spencer and Jones, Oklahoma. I knew the blessings of God were upon me.

While coming home late Friday evening, I made a wonderful discovery after getting lost. I was trying to get home without a road map. When one is lost, ask someone for proper directions. Every lost person who wants salvation is asking the same question that the Philippian

Jailer asked, in **Acts 16:30, "And brought them out, and said, Sirs, what must I do to be saved?"** Jesus Christ is truly our road map and the subject of evangelism.

After my wife Joyce, graduated from college, she and our Daughter Dee Dee returned to Denver with me. We were blessed with a house to rent through the cook at the camp where I worked.

As I stated previously, I thought we made the move to Denver for our wealth and good fortune. Little did I know, that God was preparing me for my future ministry.

It would be a ministry dealing with young people, street people, and those that are sometimes classified as the poor underprivileged. I was learning my lesson in bits and pieces and receiving a preview of my good works to come. Yet, God was not through with me.

After working with the Juvenile System for six months, I knew I had to find something different, because the odd hours kept me away from my family, and I was not making a fortune either. I found a job, or God gave me a new position totally out of my field. I was selling cars for Burt's Chevrolet Dealership. Guess What? It was in Littleton, Colorado where I bought my RT Dodge Coronet.

Our blessings are not far from us. Sometimes they are down the street, and at other times, they are up the street. Sometimes they are around the corner, but, they are never far from where God the Father has you. With this job, God gave me the opportunity to work with a different group of people, from the other side of the track.

The only things I had sold, in the past, were seeds to neighbors in my community as a boy. This was quite a challenge from selling garden seeds. The car sales position built my confidence, self-esteem, and exposed me to the operations of a business. It also taught me endurance and how to acknowledge disappointments. There were times, that a great Saturday turned into a disastrous Monday, because Saturday's deals could be not financed.

As head of my household, not only did I know that I was to provide, for the physical and emotional needs of my family, but also the spiritual, as well. God began to deal with me about finding a church home. I had one problem. I could not find my home church, the Church of the Living God, the Pillar and Ground of the Truth in Denver, Colorado. There were none then.

God brought me into a spiritual awareness that my belief in the Lord Jesus Christ was what saved me. It had nothing to do with a denomination and the name of the church house nailed on the building.

I have learned since, that God is not impressed with anyone but the Lord Jesus Christ. He is the Way, the Truth, and the Life, and truly no man can come to the Father, but by Him. We should lift up Jesus Christ as the Son of the Living God, who was born of a virgin and lived a sinless life. He died a vicarious substitutional death for our sins, and rose again on the third day according to the scriptures. He ascended to the right hand of the Father and is Lord of Lords with all authority in heaven and in earth.

If we point men to Christ Jesus, we will be accomplishing the mandate of the church. However, I am afraid that typically the Church has deviated and made everything other than Jesus Christ the subject of evangelism. We have made the pulpit, the building, and the choir more important. There is more emphasis placed on the money raised, the convention, the fashions, and the office held. Even banquets, and members of the church have been made the primary attractions for the unchurched.

We note plainly in **Romans 10:9,13, "That if thou shalt confess with thy mouth the Lord Jesus, and shalt believe in thine heart that God hath raised him from the dead, thou shalt be saved." "For whosoever shall call upon the name of the Lord shall be saved."**

We have further evidence of this Divine truth in the following scriptures:

> **I Corinthians 15: 1-4, "Moreover, brethren, I declare unto you the gospel which I preached unto you, which also ye have received, and wherein ye stand; By which also ye are saved, if ye keep in memory what I preached unto you, unless ye have believed in vain. For I delivered unto you first of all that which I also received, how that Christ died for our sins according to the scriptures; and that he was buried, and that he rose again the third day according to the scriptures:"**

For in Christ, **"There is one body, and one Spirit, even as ye are called in one hope of your calling; One Lord, one faith, one baptism, One God and Father of all, who is above all, and through all, and in you all." Ephesians 4:4-6.**

While searching for a church home, we visited one of the largest churches in Denver. We wanted to feel welcomed, but not one person spoke to us. The church did not display friendliness or love.

Many people are lost from membership and salvation through improper welcoming of visitors or guests in local churches. Many times we fail to evangelize and capitalize on the people God sends us in our own backyards. We should show every visitor that comes to the local church love and hospitality. Someone in the church should follow up on visitors by a telephone call, a letter, or a personal visit. For this to be done, many will fall in love with God's only begotten Son and embrace Him as Savior and Lord. The church needs to convey the message of the Lord Jesus Christ, as God's Ultimate One, our only Hope of Glory.

The Work of the Holy Spirit

We continued to search for a church until we remembered that my wife's beautician Mrs. Jimmie Neece in Oklahoma gave us her sister Mrs. Willie Mae Swisher's name as a contact for our needs in Denver.

There are no accidents in relationships. Throughout the Bible, we see God dealing with us and others through relationships. Sometimes relationships lead from one house to another, but it can also mean going to the other side of town.

> **Acts 2:46, "And they, continuing daily with one accord in the temple, and breaking bread from house to house, did eat their meat with gladness and singleness of heart,"**

> **Acts 20:20, "And how I kept back nothing that was profitable unto you, but have showed you, and have taught you publicly, and from house to house,"**

We need always to remember that relationships lead us from house to house, but not necessarily in a systematic way. Sharing the good news of Jesus Christ will lead us from one relative or friend to another. The evangelist in every saved person has a desire to see their relatives and friends saved. God gave me the opportunity to evangelize some of my sisters and brothers. Many of my friends have received the Lord Jesus Christ through God using me to evangelize them. True evangelism starts at home and spreads throughout our community.

I am grateful to God for the knowledge of knowing that my paternal and maternal grandparents were saved. It is a comfort to know that, my parents, wife, children, brothers, sisters, uncles, aunts, close friends, close neighbors, and other relatives are saved. The harvest is your kin, family, and friends. Saved people's relationships have eternal significance.

> **Matthew 4:18-22, "And Jesus, walking by the sea of Galilee, saw two brethren, Simon called Peter, and Andrew his brother, casting a net into the sea: for they were fishers. And he saith unto them, Follow me, and I will make you fishers of men. And they straightway left their nets, and followed him. And going on from thence, he saw other two brethren, James the son of Zebedee, and John his brother, in a ship with Zebedee their father, mending their nets; and he called them. And they immediately left the ship and their father, and followed him."**

We also see in John 1:40-45:

"One of the two which heard John speak, and followed him, was Andrew, Simon Peter's brother. He first findeth his own brother Simon, and saith unto him, We have found the Messias, which is, being interpreted, the Christ. And he brought him to Jesus. And when Jesus beheld him, he said, Thou art Simon the son of Jona: thou shalt be called Cephas, which is by interpretation, A stone. The day following Jesus would go forth into Galilee, and findeth Philip, and saith unto him, Follow me. Now Philip was of Bethsaida, the city of Andrew and Peter. Philip findeth Nathanael, and saith unto him, We have found him, of whom Moses in the law, and the prophets, did write, Jesus of Nazareth, the son of Joseph."

We relied upon relationships in Denver, Colorado. Upon contacting Mrs. Swisher, she helped us find a baby-sitter. She invited my wife to come and volunteer to work in her church, Mt. Gilead Baptist Church where Dr. Acen Phillips was Pastor. We eventually united with the Mt. Gilead Baptist Church, approximately two months before returning to Oklahoma. Sometimes our job is just to get a person going in the right direction, then our work is finished. We should never feel rejected about this part of God's ministry. Often, believers need to go by at least three to four local assemblies before God settles them at a local assembly.

Remember to hold everything and everyone loosely, for they all are on loan. Through these events, my spiritual awareness was broadened. I was awakened concerning salvation for all, and realized Christianity reaches beyond denominations. It taught me something about the love of God for the world.

John 3:16, "For God so loved the world, that he gave his only begotten Son, that whosoever believeth in him should not perish, but have everlasting life."

I now know that it was the Holy Spirit, who was leading, guiding, and orchestrating every situation. True evangelism can never be done apart from the empowerment and direction of the Holy Spirit.

God's Will Must Be Discovered

Returning to Oklahoma, we realized home was not so bad after all, especially since it was in God's will. We became a part of the St. James Baptist Church where my wife had been a member.

God gives us our desires according to His will, and we end up fulfilling His will because of our desires. It was the desire of both my wife and Pastor Parker that we would come to the Loving St. James Baptist Church after our marriage. Yet, I am grateful to God that she allowed me to be the head of our household. Although her heart was still at St. James, she followed me to my church. All married couples should seek God for the one church, the one banking account, and the one household.

God progressively gets us where He wants us through relationships and the Holy Spirit. Again, God reminded me of the plan He had for my life. Pastor Parker was my agriculture teacher in high school. Never would I have imagined that Mr. Parker, "Buddy," as we called him, would be my Pastor. He was a Pastor doing the work of an Evangelist and a son, in the gospel, of Rev. H.A. Walker, who inspired him to evangelize.

According to II Timothy 4:5, "But watch thou in all things, endure afflictions, do the work of an evangelist, make full proof of thy ministry."

This type of ministry was very inspirational to me. After ten years of running, saying no to God the Father, I surrendered to preach in November of 1970. The announcement was made after great conviction had come. It was during the Sunday School review of Isaiah 6:1ff by Pastor W.B. Parker. I finally said, "Yes Lord, here am I, send me." I thank God for helping me to yield to His call. I thank God for helping me to remain faithful to my call. Although there have been times I felt like giving up, God helped me to remember the call. A true call from God will sustain you when nothing else will.

"This is the day which the LORD hath made; we will rejoice and be glad in it."

This poem, I suppose, expresses the feelings of many men of God.

I'LL NEVER LET GO

I want to let go
But I won't let go
There are battles to fight
By day and by night
For God and the right
And I'll never let go.
I want to let go
But I won't let go.
I'm sick, Tis True
Worried and blue
And worn through and through
I want to let go
But I won't let go.
I will never yield.
What? Lie down on the field
And surrender my shield?
No, I'll never let go.
I want to let go
But I won't let go.
May this be my song
Mid legions of wrong
Oh, God keep me strong
That I may never let go.

(Anonymous)

Poem given by: Dr. S. Tatum, Southwestern Theological Seminary, Fort Worth, Texas

It is my prayer that every believer of the Lord Jesus Christ will never let go. You see, the world needs a preacher before it can come to know the redeeming grace of God. There is no wonder Paul declared in **Romans 10:14-15:**

> **Romans 10:14,15, "How then shall they call on him in whom they have not believed? and how shall they believe in him of whom they have not heard? and how shall they hear without a preacher? And how shall they preach, except they be sent? as it is written, How beautiful are the feet of them that preach the gospel of peace, and bring glad tidings of good things !"**

I discovered in the early part of my ministry that God had gifted me to be an evangelist. There is a vast difference in pastors or teachers serving as evangelist and those called and equipped to be an evangelist. In many churches, the gift of evangelist has been overlooked. Maybe this is the reason so many young preachers are sitting and waiting for a church, rather than doing evangelistic work.

In **Matthew 9:37**, Jesus Christ declares **"Then saith he unto his disciples, The harvest truly is plenteous, but the labourers are few;"** No one should be waiting for an opportunity to preach, or minister when the harvest is so plenteous. God has a place and a work for every true man of God willing to do His will, and often, the job is being an evangelist. In some circles the role of an evangelist is extremely challenging, but if we are to reign with Him, we must suffer for Him.

If God is calling you to be an evangelist, do it. God's will is sweeter than anything you can imagine. The Lord will see you through regardless of the difficulties. In my personal experience as an Evangelist, receiving ministerial recognition and support was extremely difficult at first, because the gift of an evangelist was not encouraged, exercised, or recognized like God intended, in the African American community. This is the reason we are only doing a nominal job in evangelizing the world to Christ. Our young preachers and young people should be encouraged to become evangelists and missionaries. They should be given the support and recognition needed to be successful, fruitful, productive men and women of God.

If it is God, any evangelistic work should complement and be in conjunction with the church, because God really uses the church. God is sovereign and has the right to give gifts to the Church. Every gift of God is of ultimate significance for the well-being of the Body of Christ. The Initiator of Evangelism has a purpose, plan, call, and will for reaching the world for Christ.

Let us conform to God's will and fulfill His desires by being obedient to His Word. Note the words from Dr. Luke concerning the greatest Evangelist that ever lived, and still lives.

> **Luke 19: 10, "For the Son of man is come to seek and to save that which was lost."**

Pictured left is Pastor Jayel Jacobs, Jr. with his friends at, "The Church of the Living God, The Pillar and Ground of the Truth" pictured below.

Dunjee Independents

***Front Row:** H. Moses, C. Patton, J. Ellis, C. Lewis, W. Henderson,*
***Second Row:** C. Cash, J. Jacobs Jr., E. Lewis, H. Baker, C. Wright*
***Third Row:** Coaches: J. Jacobs Sr., N. Lewis, J. Cash, L. Patton*
***Not Shown:** A. Stewart, W. L. Parker, and R. Anderson*

Pictured above are the Street Ministry Members and below are the children who attended the Street Ministry Study House.

Chapter Two

Evangelism In Action - Something You Do!

Evangelism is not something you warehouse, but something you do. One can best learn how to evangelize by doing it. Evangelism is God working in us both to will and to do of His good pleasure.

Warehousing is learning how to share the good news of Jesus Christ with lost people, but never getting around to it. This is what is meant in **II Timothy 3:7, "Ever learning, and never able to come to the knowledge of the truth."** Many study, but are not putting into action what they have learned. Some are preaching it, but not living it; teaching it, but not doing it; singing about it, but not sharing it; and studying it, but not practicing it. This is happening at churches everywhere, at seminars, workshops, evangelistic conferences, conventions, and seminaries. Warehousing evangelism must cease and real evangelism must begin.

One day while witnessing from door-to-door in the Oklahoma City area, although I did not know it then, I entered a house tavern. As I began sharing the gospel with the people present in the house, a man came from a back room in a wheelchair. He began to curse God and me while I was kneeling in prayer. I stopped praying and began to rebuke Satan in the man. It seemed to me that it made him worse. The Holy Spirit then commanded me to go over to the man and tell him that I loved him and also to hug him. The man broke down and cried. I had a chance to share the love of Christ not only with him, but also with the others who were in the house. I realized through this encounter, that God was working with me to evangelize my city, or Jerusalem.

Love Is Imperative

We can never accomplish effective evangelism apart from the love of Christ flowing from a yielded vessel, in the hands of the Holy Spirit. God exemplified His love by sending His Son, the Lord Jesus, to the world to pay the sin debt for humanity. The Lord Jesus manifested His love to the Father and humanity by laying down His life that others might live. The Father sent the Holy Spirit to pour the love of Christ in every believer, that we may illustrate the charity of God the Father in reaching the world for Christ. Since He has shown His love for us, we ought to show love for others and witness of this love to them. Many of us are calling Him Lord, Lord, and not doing a thing to fulfill the great commission. Something is seriously wrong with a person who claims a personal relationship with Jesus Christ and does not evangelize.

Jesus poses this question, **"And why call ye me, Lord, Lord, and do not the things which I say?" St. Luke 6:46.** If we truly love God, and we are grateful to Him, we will go. Jesus declares to us, **"If ye love me, keep my commandments." John 14:15**

> **John 21:15-17, "So when they had dined, Jesus saith to Simon Peter, Simon, son of Jonas, lovest thou me**

more than these? He saith unto him, Yea, Lord; thou knowest that I love thee. He saith unto him, Feed my lambs.

He saith to him again the second time, Simon, son of Jonas, lovest thou me? He saith unto him, Yea, Lord; thou knowest that I love thee. He saith unto him, Feed my sheep.

He saith unto him the third time, Simon, son of Jonas, lovest thou me? Peter was grieved because he said unto him the third time, Lovest thou me? And he said unto him, Lord, thou knowest all things; thou knowest that I love thee. Jesus saith unto him, Feed my sheep."

Love for Him will get the job done. **I John 4:16 LB**

"We know how much God loves us because we have felt this love and because we believe him when he tells us that he loves us dearly. God is love, and anyone who lives in love is living with God and God is living in him."

I Corinthians 13:7, "Beareth all things, believeth all things, hopeth all things, endureth all things."

God has specific instructions about what we should do. He commands us to, **"Go ye therefore, and teach all nations, baptizing them in the name of the Father, and of the Son, and of the Holy Ghost: Teaching them to observe all things whatsoever I have commanded you: and, lo, I am with you alway, even unto the end of the world. Amen"** ***Matthew 28:19-20***

Love for Him will find a way to obey this great mandate. Have you seen anyone lately in love with Christ?

I John 4:9-11, "In this was manifested the love of God toward us, because that God sent his only begotten

> **Son into the world, that we might live through him. Herein is love, not that we loved God, but that he loved us, and sent his Son to be the propitiation for our sins. Beloved, if God so loved us, we ought also to love one another."**

In every evangelistic endeavor that you undertake, you should allow the love of God, produced by the Holy Spirit, to govern you in making disciples. Evangelize your city, state, surrounding states, and the world. A deep love for God the Father and the Lord Jesus Christ moved me to do and to go many places that were insane in the natural.

I am reminded of the words of St. Paul in **I Corinthians 4:10-14:**

> **"We are fools for Christ's sake, but ye are wise in Christ; we are weak, but ye are strong; ye are honourable, but we are despised.**
>
> **Even unto this present hour we both hunger, and thirst, and are naked, and are buffeted, and have no certain dwelling place; And labour, working with our own hands: being reviled, we bless; being persecuted, we suffer it: Being defamed, we entreat: we are made as the filth of the world, and are the offscouring of all things unto this day.**
>
> **I write not these things to shame you, but as my beloved sons I warn you."**

God's love for the world has not changed. Since love lives in every Christian's heart, love will then express itself in the love we have for others. Love never fails!

While witnessing one day on the corner of 7th and Harrison, in Oklahoma City, Oklahoma a man asked me,

"If I cut you, will you bleed?" My reply was, "Yes". I continued to tell him that I fell in love with him the moment I saw him. He immediately repented and asked me to forgive him. I discovered through this experience that God's love will always prevail. We must love people to evangelize them, whether loved ones, or foes. Love for God the Father and His Son will fix much of the disobedience in the church today.

Evangelism Targets The Lost

Pastor Parker showed me how to evangelize by precept and example. One Christmas evening, we went out preaching and witnessing in the Fred Factory Gardens Apartments in Parker Heights.

Pastor Parker was preaching and I was witnessing to a young man, for a good while. Pastor Parker sensed that something was wrong and approached us. The young man began to cry so profusely, that we had to get under his shoulders and carry him to his apartment. We began to share the plan of salvation with him. To our amazement, he took out a gun, unloaded it, and placed it on a coffee table. He told us that he had sworn to God that if he had found his wife that night, he was going to kill her. Instead, he accepted Christ.

It is good for a young preacher to have an experienced pastor, evangelist, missionary, or teacher, as a mentor to disciple him. Often it may seem to a young minister that it is a waste of time to sit, listen, and learn from an experienced man or woman of God. However, observation will teach you many things and will help you in becoming productive and wise. It has been said that, "Birds of a feather flock together." To learn from and fellowship with a strong committed pastor or evangelist gives safety, protection, and deliverance from many harmful pitfalls of the ministry. These include: the love for money, immorality, improper desire for power, pride, envy, jealousy, and gossip.

Evangelism is truly learned by doing. It goes beyond studying, researching, and warehousing. Many evangelists and pastors are attempting to encourage others to evangelize without doing it themselves in a personal way. Even at the age of 22, it did not take me long to figure out Pastor Parker's priority.

Evangelizing is something you learn and do, mostly outside the four walls of God's House. It is not inviting Christians, who are already saved, to come to the Lord. It is not building up other Christians in the Lord only. Grandma used to say, "It is for those out of the ark of safety, and for those who have not accepted the Lord Jesus Christ, while the blood runs warm in their veins."

I discovered, in my arena, that many Christians in the early seventies did not know that they were saved or how to tell others how to come to Christ. A systematic method of presenting God's plan of salvation had never been taught for many, nor did they have the assurance of their own salvation. Some had only a form of godliness and did not have a personal relationship, or a born again experience with Jesus Christ. The lost, many times are in your home and in the pews of many churches. This is the reason we should always give the gospel at every opportunity.

While in Dallas, Texas evangelizing, Rev. Stacy Cowan introduced me to the Christian Life New Testament. I began to share a systematic approach of the good news of Christ, according to one of the master outlines. I noticed that most people I dealt with did not read well or like to read, especially wordy material. So, I wrote a short, easy to read evangelistic tract to give to receptive prospects.

God made me know that many Christians did not share the good news of Jesus Christ from the Bible because they did not know how. Many had been told, but not taught how to witness or share their faith. The Lord used me to write a step-by-step witnessing approach and follow-up booklet to show others how the Lord had led me to tell others of our faith. After becoming a pastor, God used me to design witnessing cards with symbols to simplify the presentation of Christ. Later, I made some witnessing videos on evangelism to show and explain how to evangelize, witness, or proclaim the gospel of Jesus Christ. I have not only led others to Christ, but have shown many how to fish for men through the direct or indirect approach that the Lord gave me.

We have spent many hours training and preparing others on how to witness, what to say, what not to say, what to do, and what not to do. Through in-house role-play, many have been equipped to do the work of the ministry. Role-play gives a feeling of a realistic situation, making it easier when going into the field sharing the gospel.

I started going out with my Pastor street preaching, witnessing, and visiting. I started working with several young preachers: Rev. Calvino Muse, Rev. Cliet Wilburn,

Rev. Carl Douglas, and Rev. Raymond Wandick going from corner to corner, community to community, church to church, and preaching in youth revivals. The churches that allowed us to preach were: the Hillwood Baptist Church, Pastor, Rev. O.B. Burrough, the Pilgrim Rest Baptist Church, Pastor, Rev. M.L. Tucker, the First Baptist Church of Green Pastures, Pastor, Rev. A.A. Bolten, and others who allowed us to grow-up at their expense.

I later worked with the Youth for Christ Fellowship, along with Pastor Willie Boone, Jr., Pastor J.D. Ford, Pastor A.W. Tubbs, Pastor G. Spriggs, and Pastor L.C. Jacobs. We were able to get some of the young people to go witnessing and street preaching by going with them. As a result, the Street Ministry Inc. was born and organized in 1974 with some of the same young people as members and searchers for lost people, especially in the black community. A ministry other than the church was not the norm then. The Street Ministry worked with churches in evangelizing the world to Jesus Christ by majoring in finding the lost and making disciples for the Lord Jesus from the streets, communities, and churches.

As I was witnessing one day, I remember driving down 2nd Street, 7th and Harrison, and 13th and Walnut Street wondering who was going to major in ministering daily to the spiritual needs of those people who were sometimes termed as, "Street People." The Lord was quick to respond, "You will," and brought me under conviction to be that needed man who would leave God's house and go into the fields and work.

At that time, I was working at Kraft Foods, Inc. as a sales representative. It was a great career opportunity, however, the Lord had laid on my heart to go full-time as an Evangelist. He led me to preach on the streets not only in Oklahoma City, but throughout the United States. He gave me specific cities and states to go to, such as: Nebraska, Ohio, Texas, Michigan, New York, Los Angeles, Alabama, Mississippi, Illinois, California, and Georgia.

After much prayer, with my immediate family, our Pastor, and my Dad, we made the choice to do what the Lord was calling us to do. Our decision as a family was to go into an evangelistic ministry. While praying with us, Pastor W.B. Parker of the St. James Baptist Church and Rev. H.A. Walker of the Truevine Independent Baptist Church, along with the Holy Spirit separated me for the work of an evangelist. They also gave me $900.00 at a Dedication Service, prayed for me, and gave me their blessings in my new good work.

> **Ephesians 2:10, "For we are his workmanship, created in Christ Jesus unto good works, which God hath before ordained that we should walk in them."**

My starting monthly support totaled $178.75. Our church, St. James Baptist Church, gave me $150.00 and I received a $28.75 allotment from my younger brother, Walter C. Jacobs.

I became a full time Evangelist in 1974 and Director of the Street Ministry, Inc., after resigning from my sales position with Kraft Foods. It was extremely trying the first nine months, especially from a financial view. I had publicized that I would be a full-time Evangelist available for workshops and revivals.

I discovered that the body of Christ was not as excited as I was about my evangelistic journey. The only opportunities at that time were preaching on the streets and witnessing in the community. I went through depression and began to struggle as to whether it was God or me deciding to go full-time. I could not understand why engagements or doors were not opening.

At times, I was so depressed that I could not audibly pray, but could only moan in the Spirit. In despair, and out of anger, I decided to get a part-time job as a security officer. Christmas was approaching and I did not have anything or much money for my family. I became a night security officer, justifying my decision by saying, I would have more quiet time and would be able to study more. The truth of the matter was, I lacked faith in God.

I went to prayer meeting the following Wednesday and Pastor Parker dealt with faith. I repented and informed him that I would give my supervisor a two-week notice and quit my job. I did just that after working four days with the company.

In December of 1974, the Lord used Dr. W.K. Jackson to invite me to speak the third Sunday at St. John Missionary Baptist Church. Dr. Jackson, along with the St. John Missionary Baptist Church gave me a large offering and their endorsement. Through this experience, doors began to open from within the body of believers all over the city.

Dr. W.K. Jackson had an enormous impact upon me and my ministry. I will always be thankful to God for such a great man of God and church, who allowed me to practice on them for years in weekly revival meetings. They supported both the Street Ministry and our existing church work. There is a need today for unselfish men of God, as Dr. W.K. Jackson, who will befriend and help a wandering and despairing young man of God. God has a way and a man, for a true man of God, if you will not quit.

Support began coming in from St. John Missionary Baptist Church, the Concerned Clergy for Spiritual Renewal, the Progressive Oklahoma State Baptist Convention, Southwest Baptist Church, other churches, and Christian individuals. I became so busy that I can remember one year preaching 60 days straight in different Christian settings.

Now that the Street Ministry was firmly established, in addition to my work as Street Preacher, we began conducting crusades. We launched our first crusade in Arcadia, Oklahoma. We used the old school gymnasium, and preached on the streets throughout the city. From this type of setting, we went door to door witnessing, street preaching, conducting revivals, and performing evangelistic workshops as the Lord saw fit. We later went on radio stations and took evangelistic tours throughout the United States.

When we were not on the street preaching and witnessing, the Street Ministry Inc., consisting of members of local churches came together for one common purpose. Our goal was winning the lost to the Lord Christ Jesus, and to disciple the new converts. We referred them to local churches for membership after they were saved. We started a bus ministry in parts of the northeast section. We brought in more than 100 children and teenagers each Monday to the Study House, to learn more about the Word of God.

Evangelism Is Training Others To Evangelize

The Lord led me throughout the streets of Oklahoma City for the lost, and to find a house for the Street Ministry. The house was to be used as headquarters and study house for the Street Ministry, Inc. God will truly direct your path in every aspect of your life if you let him. I found a house at 145 East Park Place, as the Lord had me driving throughout the city looking, early one weekday morning. The Holy Spirit led me to a nineteen-room house that needed extensive work. As I entered the house, the Holy Spirit leaped within me with joy and I knew I had discovered the house He wanted us to have as a ministry.

It was owned by Mr. Wendell Phillips. I had only one problem—— no money. Nevertheless, God, my Father is rich and supplied our need. Mr. Phillips financed the house for $10,000, took a tax write off of $3,000, and a $500 down payment. Many financial things were done by assuming an original note, or getting the owner to carry the note with a reasonable down payment. This was the beginning of the Street Ministry Study House and Headquarters for learning, training, teaching, and making disciples of the people won on the streets and in the community. We taught them to share with others after we led them to the Lord. We referred them to local churches according to relationships and their geographical location. Evangelism is learned by doing, not by warehousing.

The church has to walk away from the worship celebration saying more than, “We had a good time”. It has to experience miracles within its midst and the greatest miracle that can take place is a born again experience from above in a lost person. This cannot take place without doing evangelism. Not talking about it, singing about it, preaching about it, teaching about it, or warehousing it, but doing it.

Seen above, some members of the Northeast Project, an organized group of churches, sponsored a "Parade Against Crime" involving the community, civic groups, and schools. Street preaching and personal evangelism took place along the way resulting in some believing on the Lord Jesus Christ.

History

The following is the History of the Street Ministry Inc., organized by Evangelist Jacobs in 1974.

The beginning of the Street Ministry, Inc. was predestined by the Lord, in that He brought a group of young people together with the same ultimate love, desire, and compassion for lost souls. On December 28, 1973, these young people met for prayer meeting. It was through this prayer session that the Lord began to reveal His plan and purpose to us. The Lord chose Evangelist Jayel Jacobs, Jr. to organize the Street Ministry. He was greatly inspired by his Pastor, Rev. Willie B. Parker, who had consistently led him and others on the street to preach and witness for several years.

In March 1974 under the direction of the Holy Spirit, Evangelist Jayel Jacobs, Jr., left his job with Kraft Foods, Co. as a sales representative to devote himself full time to the winning of souls. In April 1974 Rev. Willie B. Parker, Pastor of St. James Baptist Church, and the members expressed their love, concern, and support to Evangelist Jayel Jacobs, Jr. and family by launching an Evangelist Appreciation for him, acknowledging his call to this work.

The Street Ministry was incorporated on April 24, 1974 as a nondenominational nonprofit organization and was federally exempt. This document was signed by our Board of Directors: Evangelist Jayel Jacobs, Jr., Rev. Cliet Wilburn, and Sis. Shirley Nero. Our headquarters was located at 1428 Alan Lane in Midwest City, Oklahoma. Guidelines were set for the ministry in taking the Word of God to the people. They were: believing in the inspired Word of God, the Bible, the Trinity of God, the Deity of Jesus Christ, the Deity

of the Holy Ghost, and the absolute necessity of the new birth in order to be a Christian.

The ultimate scope of this ministry is that the Word of God will be spread nationally and internationally. We have preached on the streets in Oklahoma, Texas, Kansas, Colorado, Missouri, Mississippi, and Tennessee.

Our second crusade was in Chandler, Oklahoma May 1974. There were 30 people to accept Christ as their Saviour. A fifteen minute program was initiated on June 30, 1974 with KBYE from 10:15 to 10:30, but was rescheduled and we are now broadcasting from KFJL Sunday mornings at 7:30 a.m. until 7:45 a.m.

In June of 1974, a crusade was held in Arcadia, Oklahoma; 25 accepted Christ. A Statewide Crusade was held at the Civic Center, Oklahoma City, Oklahoma on November 21-23, 1974; 35 accepted Christ.

At the beginning of this ministry we met from house to house, but on June 10, 1975 a house located at 145 East Park Place, Oklahoma City, Oklahoma, was purchased for the purpose of a Headquarters and Study house. The first days in the Study House were spent renovating, praying, and giving of thanks.

The Study House is not designed to take the place of a local assembly, but to work closely with pastors and churches as a referring agent for new converts; to work with any members of a particular church or denomination in making better witnesses and disciples; to help establish witnessing programs in local churches throughout the United States; to make disciples out of believers, and to set up Bible Study Classes. Our ultimate objective and purpose is soul winning and discipleship.

We have worked with churches in revival services and conducted workshops. Over the months, the Lord has laid on the hearts of these churches to support us in

this ministry. They are: Morning Star Baptist Church, Anadarko, Oklahoma, Rev. Leroy Davis, Pastor; Union Missionary Baptist Church, Shawnee, Oklahoma, Rev. Cliet Wilburn, Pastor; St. John Baptist Church, Oklahoma City, Oklahoma, Rev. W.K. Jackson, Pastor; and St. James Baptist Church, Spencer, Oklahoma, Rev. Willie B. Parker, Pastor.

Recent supporters are: Baptist Ministers Association, Rev. J. B. Bratton, Jr., President; The Concerned Clergy for Spiritual Renewal, Rev. M.A. Curry, President; Oklahoma Baptist State Convention, Rev. T.O. Chappelle, Sr., President; Progressive Oklahoma Baptist State Convention, Inc., Rev. W.K. Jackson, President.

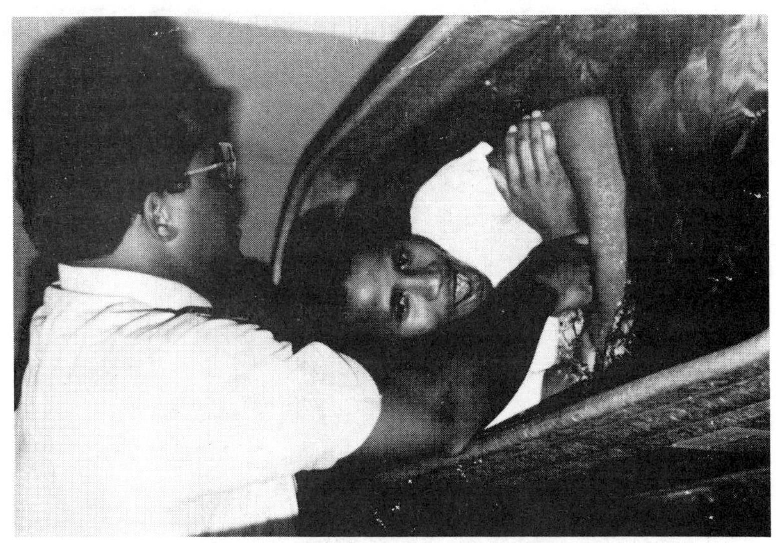

Pastor Jacobs is baptizing a new convert in 1979 in a "horse trough", which was used as a baptistry. This took place at the Street Ministry Inc. Headquarters and Study House which the Church was using at that time.

Pastor Jacobs and others at a Del City Missionary Baptist Church service meeting at 145 East Park Place.

At the beginning of Christian Life's establishment, this is a view of people coming at invitation. 15-20 people would come on any given Sunday.

Pastor Jacobs ministering in the sanctuary of what is now the Willie Wilson Fellowship Hall.

Chapter Three
Evangelism Requires A Teacher

After three years of working with Kraft Foods Company, God led me into a full-time evangelistic work. Being full-time for about four months, I discovered that it was not going as I had anticipated it would. As an Evangelist, times were very hard. I can remember once my wife, two children, and I had run out of food except for spices. Before going to work that morning my wife asked, "What are we going to eat this evening?" I replied, "It is not time to eat yet." During the early part of the afternoon God sent three bags of groceries by Shirley Williams, a member of the Street Ministry and supplied our needs. She did not know our present situation. From that experience, I learned that the Lord had not forsaken us and would meet every need.

> **Hebrews 13:5, " . . . I will never leave thee, nor forsake thee."**

Whatever God calls one to do, He promised to supply all needs according to His riches in glory. I am a living witness He is trustworthy. Do not be afraid to step out on His Word and evangelize.

The Lord Will Direct Your Path

After about eight and a half years of doing evangelistic work, I realized that the Lord was leading me into a Pastoral Ministry. Through much prayer, I discovered the will of

God for my life. He was leading me to become a full-time Pastor.

> **"And I will give you pastors according to mine heart, which shall feed you with knowledge and understanding." (Jeremiah 3:15)**

I guess I had inclinations of being a pastor about two years before it happened. I honestly had no desire to be a pastor after I entered full-time evangelistic work. We need always remember that God has the right to do as He pleases with our lives. Our responsibility is to follow His loving Divine leadership without doubt or hesitation. The best candidates for the job are the ones who are chosen.

While attending Southwestern Theological Seminary and being a part-time Evangelist, the Lord made it plain to me, that He wanted me to be a pastor, doing the work of an evangelist. He reminded me through His Word that saints needed equipping for the work of the ministry. This requires more extensive teaching and training in evangelism. He revealed to me that I could, with Him, do a greater work as a pastor. Every call of God is always a promotion. According to **Ephesians 4:11-12:**

> **"And he gave some, apostles; and some, prophets; and some, evangelists; and some, pastors and teachers; For the perfecting of the saints, for the work of the ministry, for the edifying of the body of Christ:"**

and

> **II Timothy 2:2, "And the things that thou hast heard of me among many witnesses, the same commit thou to faithful men, who shall be able teach others also."**

Evangelism requires a teacher who can influence God's people to become faithful and committed to the things of God, and that includes evangelizing the world to Jesus Christ. As the Lord instructed, we organized the First African American Church of Del City, Oklahoma with my wife and two children. I do realize that in Christ Jesus, there is neither black, white, red, nor yellow.

> **Galatians 3:28. "There is neither Jew nor Greek, there is neither bond nor free, there is neither male nor female: for ye are all one in Christ Jesus."**

We held our first service in the community center in Del City and eight united in the first service. The Lord has continued to add to His church since that day. We have witnessed many astronomical miracles of God working in our midst, both willing and doing of His good pleasure.

God had now given me the privilege to win and disciple His new people in depth. Day and night we labored with the work that God had assigned us with His help to do. I went to school day by day, sometimes driving back and forth from Ft.Worth, Texas. Preaching in revival meetings and studying by night, we were fulfilling God's purpose.

God's will is not always convenient, however, it is always rewarding, fruitful, and joyful. Sacrifices were made and must be made to have great ministries. Sometimes working by day and night not only gives the appearance of instability in the mind, but also of evil intent. Not only did I do this, but I also taught others to do the same. Let God be the Judge.

> **Mark 3:21, "And when his friends heard of it, they went out to lay hold on him: for they said, He is beside himself."**

> **Mark 3:22, "And the scribes which came down from Jerusalem said, He hath Beelzebub, and by the prince of the devils casteth he out devils."**

I began my pastoral ministry of evangelism with a deep commitment of obtaining all the goals that I believed the Holy Spirit was leading me to reach. Every church and church auxiliary should set people and financial goals.

> **Luke 1:37, "For with God nothing shall be impossible."**

A committed person in Christ, led by the Holy Spirit, will often be misunderstood. This is just the way it is! I want to encourage everyone to do what God calls them to do, despite the cost. When you cannot do it for others, do it for the cause of Christ.

There are no limitations in what can be done for the glory of Christ. There has to be consistent preaching, teaching, training, planning, and praying for spiritual growth. This must be done whether individually or collectively. It is work!

> **I Corinthians 15:10, "But by the grace of God I am what I am: and his grace which was bestowed upon me was not in vain; but I laboured more abundantly than they all: yet not I, but the grace of God which was with me."**

A name for our church was needed, so we called ourselves the Del City Missionary Baptist Church. Soon after, we purchased 2 ½ acres of land on S.E. Bryant in Del City, Oklahoma. This was the place where "we thought" God was leading us to build His house. We later sold the land because it was not sufficient for our needs. It is God that always gives the increase to His church. He's powerful!

> **Acts 2:41, "Then they that gladly received his word were baptized: and the same day there were added unto them about three thousands souls.**

Always remember the Lord can and does what pleases Him. I have witnessed in my personal ministry the Lord adding one to twenty people to our church, in a morning worship experience. I have witnessed thousands coming to the Lord on the streets in Oklahoma City, Oklahoma, Dallas, Texas, Jackson, Mississippi, Atlanta, Georgia, Chicago, Illinois, Cincinnati, Ohio, and other cities across America.

Approximately a year before the Atlanta murders, God had me preaching in complexes and trouble spots in that city. I warned men to repent and turn to the Lord Jesus before it was too late! I saw more men come to Christ in Atlanta than any other city I had ever preached.

We have witnessed baptizing new converts every Sunday for years. After a youth evangelistic drama organized and written by my Daughter Deya and some youth of the church, we baptized forty-seven. I can recall on a Wednesday night after prayer meeting, baptizing fifty-three of God's people. Now, back to the story.

The nineteen room house the Lord had given us was getting crowded. We used the basement and all three floors to teach the Word of God. The first floor was the sanctuary.

We had people in the entrance of the house, in the kitchen of the house, and in the Pastor's study, which was a converted porch. The center and sides of the main floor and upstairs were also used. The former Street Ministry House and Headquarters was being used to its capacity. This house was given to the church after the Street Ministry organized our church.

It was exciting to see the mighty hand of God moving and working in the young and the old converts. We were challenging God's people to go and bring in the lost. The lost were coming and being saved and going back into the world to rescue the perishing. One advantage of being a pastor-teacher of a new work was the freedom to teach and train God's people more than just church work. We need, as pastors, to evangelize the world. Every pastor has the right to receive the freedom and the support of the local church to do, and teach others the work of the church.

Ask and Ye Shall Receive

Since the House of God and the Family of God, was growing fast, we asked God to give us a larger building according to: **Matthew 7:7, "Ask, and it shall be given you; seek, and ye shall find; knock, and it shall be open unto you:**

Dr. Bert Harrison, former Pastor of the Southwest Baptist Church of Oklahoma, was introduced to me by one of my radio listeners, Mrs. W.O. Merrill. She was a great woman of God and a true sister in the Lord. After much prayer, Dr. Harrison, Ronald Moore, and I were led by the Spirit throughout Del City and parts of Midwest City to finally arrived at 4621 N.E. 23rd Street. It had been the Providence

Nazarene Home for Boys under the leadership of Dr. Joe Edwards. After agreeing to pay more than $100,000 for the building and four acres of land, we were again thrust into a situation where we had to trust and obey God to supply the need.

We had originally organized for establishment in Del City. The Lord however, led us to purchase the property at 4621 N.E. 23rd Street in Oklahoma City. Therefore, we had to change our name. In a church meeting, Milton Holmes suggested the name of Christian Life Missionary Baptist Church. The church agreed, and adopted it.

The name of any church is providential and has great significance whether realized or not. A church's name should have an objective. Every name means something and we are the reflection of our name. We had another problem, and that was, where would we get more than a $100,000 to purchase this new property? As Pastor H.A. Walker would say, "When you need money, ask God for it."

Our Needs Will be Supplied

One responsibility of God's man is to teach God's people the ability of God to do beyond their asking or thinking. Our God is able according to: **Ephesians 3:20, "Now unto him that is able to do exceeding abundantly above all that we ask or think, according to the power that worketh in us,"**

We were encouraged by the Southwest Baptist Church who gave us our first $7,000. This motivated our church to give and believe God to meet the need. After receiving financial commitments from each member, one young man in our church took a second mortgage on his home to borrow $10,000 for the down payment on our new property.

Along with assuming some loans against the property, we were able to buy the building. We did it a fork full at a time, and that is how you eat an elephant; "A fork -full at a time." We have used this principle in our church to do some great things in the Lord.

> **According to Philippians 4:13, "I can do all things through Christ which strengtheneth me."**

Not only did God supply the knowledge and the ability in obtaining those finances, He became our ever present sufficiency and source. I give all the glory to God for giving us all we needed to get the job done. He will always supply our needs according to His will. If God is in it, He will make a way. Love will always make a way, and love for Him will always find a way to get the job done.

Success is knowing the will of God and doing it. Our Father has never let us down and He will not let you down. The biggest thing is not to talk negative, but to make a start with the Lord. When I made a start with the Lord, regardless of how large the project or obstacle, the Lord saw me through. Never think or speak defeat, always think and confess victory in Christ Jesus our Lord.

> **I Corinthians 15:57, "But thanks be to God, which giveth us the victory through our Lord Jesus Christ."**

I have learned much from my Teacher the Holy Spirit. He never leads you wrong. Nothing is too hard for God to do, if you totally depend upon Him.

Above/below buses are used to bring in children for Sunday Morning Bible Study and Children's Church.

Give, and It Shall Be Given Unto You

Not only should a young church be rooted and grounded in doing the work of the church, but they should also be rooted and grounded in giving to the church. I have noticed that it is the tendency of a new pastor to steer away from teaching biblical economics. To be a strong church the pastor must teach God's people how to give according to biblical principles.

Evangelizing effectively will be costly, especially, if you are reaching the lame, the maimed, the halt, the blind, and the poor. At one stage of my ministry, we were reaching primarily children and young adults. It was imperative that the older members knew the importance of giving so that evangelism would become a reality to others as well.

The Lord used us to start a bus ministry which was a very effective way to evangelize. Every aspect of the church had to be taught. Every pastor needs to remember we are dealing with lambs and sheep, and they need to be taught and trained by God's pastor-teacher.

We bought a fleet of used buses and began to pick up children in the community all over the city and surrounding cities. Many children and parents were saved, baptized and added to the church.

Our objective then was to reach the parents through the children. God gave us a great harvest. Many of those that, we won through door-to-door witnessing, relationships, and the bus ministry are now witnessing themselves. I have discovered people won through witnessing are more receptive to the work of an evangelist.

Teaching by Example

I was an on-the-job-teacher and I worked with our people in the field. Jesus commanded the disciples to follow Him and He would make them fishermen of men. Jesus Christ, the greatest teacher that ever lived, and lives, did on-the-job training with His disciples. To have an effective evangelistic program you must leave the confinements of the four walls of God's house and go into the world and work. It is amazing that few want to go into the market places as Jesus Christ did.

> **Mark 16:15, "And he said unto them, Go ye into all the world, and preach the gospel to every creature."**

We, as a church, began different ministries to meet the needs of God's new people. We taught the new people of God to edify the body of Christ within and reach the lost without. The marriage ministry, children's ministry, separated, divorced, & widowed ministry, single ministry, hospital ministry, prison ministry, youth ministry, carpentry ministry, and auto mechanics ministry were started because of the need to evangelize the lost.

I set up Saturday witnessing and going from door-to-door into territories. We also conducted street services in different areas of Oklahoma City. I taught that we should turn everything we did as a church into an evangelistic opportunity.

Every unique part of the church should build up the church and reach out for the lost. I performed a wedding and at the end of the ceremony, the married couple extended an invitation and the mother of the groom received the

Lord Jesus. During a single's ministry meeting, some single's were saved as the opportunity presented itself for sharing Jesus Christ's saving grace.

We started a children's church and taught the importance of evangelizing children at an early age. Many children have come to Christ during children's church. At youth meetings and youth retreats, young people accepted the Lord Jesus Christ. At funerals, countless individuals have accepted Christ because an invitation to Him was given. Once fifty-three people came to Christ at a funeral. While visiting the hospital as part of the hospital ministry, a young man was saved and is now pastoring. These are just a few examples of how we as a church have used many opportunities to win people to Christ.

Through our Sunday Morning Bible Study, we emphasized the importance of knowing and studying the word of God. I discovered if the Sunday Morning Bible Study grew then the overall church was growing and would grow. Much of our growth has come through what has been traditionally called, " The Sunday School." Christian Education always complements evangelism.

I was fortunate in the fact that God gave me the opportunity to attend and receive a Master of Religious Education Degree from Southwestern Theological Seminary in Fort Worth, Texas. I am grateful for the opportunity provided by Southern Baptists to attend Seminary. I am thankful to all of my professors for teaching me many helpful principles while there.

There were times when we were busing in 400-600 children a Sunday. There were times when one bus route would bring more than one hundred children to Sunday Morning Bible Study on a particular Sunday. This produced a space problem to the extent that we began having two services, having classes at Millwood School's Auditorium, and having classes on some of the church buses. The lack of space motivated the church to start a 1.5 million dollar building project.

Now, while all of this was developing at the Core Church, God led us to establish a mission at 145 East Park Place under the leadership of the late Carl Douglas. It later became the Living Word Missionary Baptist Church under the leadership of my eldest son in the gospel, Rev. Isaiah Sierson.

At the age of two, we established an extension from the Core Church in Edmond, Oklahoma, led by Rev. Tony Wise, and an extension in Madrid Spain, led by Rev. Bruce Jarman and Eric Davis. At the age of four, we established an extension in Norman, Oklahoma, led by Rev. Terry Wilson and Rev. Sherdeill Breathett. We also established an extension in Tulsa, Oklahoma, led by Rev. Walter Jacobs and Rev. Jimmy T. Coleman, an extension in Colorado Springs, Colorado, led by Rev. J.C. Griffin, an extension in Orlando, Florida later led by Rev. Bruce Jarman, and an extension in Goldsboro, North Carolina led by Rev. James R. Alston.

Eventually a mission in the northwest part of Oklahoma City was organized, led by Rev. Ralph Boyattia, and a mission in the far north part of Oklahoma City led by Rev. Wayne Lee and Rev. Ronald Moore. We have witnessed, by the power of God, many individuals coming and growing in the grace of God through these works.

At the age of three years old, we were in a 1.5 million dollar building program. We also purchased a building in Tulsa and another on 25th and Shartel in northwest Oklahoma City. We had started five extensions in different parts of the United States. God enabled us to support Missionaries in Mexico, China, Haiti, Africa, Brazil, Malta, Argentina, Germany, Philippines, Sicily, Spain, Japan, Ethiopia, Russia, Australia, Somalia, and the United States.

The Lord has also enabled us to give more than 1.5 million dollars to missionary endeavors throughout the history of our ministry. We are seventeen years of age now. We have spent over a quarter of a million dollars on vehicles to transport people to the house of God, and thousands of dollars on insurance, upkeep, and repairs on these vehicles.

Yes, everything had to be taught, organized, and mostly purchased by a very young church where most members had been won to the Lord through our visitation or evangelistic efforts. I truly believe in my heart that this fertile pastoral evangelistic ministry grew because we were attempting to evangelize our world and all the world. God through His power met our needs although there were times when we struggled and suffered.

> **I Corinthians 15:58, "Therefore, my beloved brethren, be ye stedfast, unmoveable, always abounding in the**

> **work of the Lord, forasmuch as ye know that your labour is not in vain in the Lord."**

Our work in the Lord according to this scripture is never unsuccessful. "Glory be to God!" Teaching by being an example is to imitate the Lord Jesus Christ. To imitate the Lord Jesus is to be successful. Teaching and evangelizing go hand in hand. Amen!

It is necessary to remember **"It Happens after Prayer"**; it **"Happens during Prayer"**, and praying and evangelizing go hand in hand.

In starting a church from scratch, I found that the new converts, who had no experience in the church, had to be taught everything. They had to be taught to love. They were also taught about the Person and work of the Lord Jesus Christ, the Holy Spirit, and His work. They needed to know what it meant to be lost, saved, led and taught by the Holy Spirit. They were taught what it means to evangelize, to study the Bible through Sunday Morning Bible Study, street preaching, giving, to do door-to-door visitation, to establish and maintain a bus ministry by territory, to pray, etc. This was true evangelism. These people had to be won and made disciples.

They were taught that there was no substitute for righteous living. A Godly lifestyle produces great dividends in the world of evangelism. Holy living produces blessings. Nothing kills a ministry and a preacher like walking in the flesh.

I had a chance to teach them the way the Lord was leading me to evangelize. As a result, we have witnessed more than 200 in prayer meeting, 888 in Sunday Morning Bible Study, and more than 150 on any given Saturday to do church visitation at the Core Church alone. We also watched the Lord add to the church every Sunday for years. We were baptizing new converts every Sunday morning and night.

We need to understand, receiving church hoppers is not true evangelism. Often these people leave their previous church or churches because of a dispute, misunderstanding or as they say, "a lack of growth," or, "being led by the Lord." Nevertheless, they are saved and just searching for a better or bigger place of worship, or for another justifiable reason. Saved people changing churches is not evangelizing the lost. We have seen many come and go, and we are thankful for the way the Lord has orchestrated our ministry. Many who walked with us were sent by the Lord throughout the world to other churches to evangelize the lost. It is the pastor's job to teach, lead, and train the people of God to evangelize, then they will lead others to Christ and make disciples.

Above is Dr. Jacobs preaching and witnessing with other members of the Progressive National Baptist Convention in Cincinnati, Ohio.

Pastor Jacobs witnessing on an evangelistic tour in one of the southern states.

Evangelist Jayel Jacobs Jr. preaching on the streets of Chicago, Illinois.

Evangelist Jayel Jacobs Jr.witnessing at a home in Jackson, Mississippi.

Chapter Four

Lessons Learned Along The Way Through Evangelism

While preaching one Saturday evening in one of the hard core spots in our city, a perplexed, very angry young man approached me. He decided to apprehend my microphone, and God only knows what else he had in mind. At that point, God sent another man from the east, who had been observing the preaching and situation nearby. He intercepted him and protected me from an assault by physically taking on the attacker. Through God's intervention, I continued preaching.

I later learned from another man by the street name of "Red" that he had a knife. He said, "If that man had touched you Reverend, I had made up in my mind to kill him, because you were not doing anything to anyone, but preaching." He began to cry, and I had an opportunity to share Christ with him. I learned through this experience the providential care of God. God will provide and protect His people even in the field.

The True Meaning of Evangelism

In Acts 1:8, "But ye shall receive power, after that the Holy Ghost is come upon you: and ye shall be witnesses unto me both in Jerusalem, and in all Judaea, and in Samaria, and unto the uttermost part of the earth."

God's plan is for us to begin at home and go to the uttermost parts of the earth. Evangelism is always, whatever your definition, "something you do." Evangelism is telling others the good news and mercies of God through the gift of His Son, the Lord Jesus Christ. This is done that others may be saved from eternal damnation. It is a fallacy to try to teach evangelism and not do it.

Key words in evangelism are going, visiting, witnessing, discipleship, follow-up, and relationships. The key persons are the Holy Spirit and you. It is not all Him, nor is it all you, but it is you working with Him in compassion for others who are lost. God always takes the initiative in evangelism according to:

> **Luke 14:23, "And the lord said unto the servant, Go out into the highways and hedges, and compel them to come in, that my house may be filled."**

Evangelism is communicating the good news of Jesus Christ's sinless life, death, burial, resurrection, and ascension, in the power of the Holy Spirit, to unsaved people, that they might receive him as Lord and Savior and in return, proclaim Him to others. Therefore, we see that the **Subject** of Evangelism is the Lord Jesus Christ. The **Benefactors** of Evangelism are unsaved people. The **Continuation** of Evangelism is through discipleship. Evangelism is a love to share the Lord Jesus with the lost, as noted in **I John 4:19; "We love him, because he first loved us."**

St. John 14:15, "If ye love me, keep my commandments."

and

I John 1:2-4, "For the life was manifested, and we have seen it, and bear witness, and shew unto you that eternal life, which was with the Father, and was manifested unto us;

That which we have seen and heard declare we unto you, that ye also may have fellowship with us: and truly our fellowship is with the Father, and with his Son Jesus Christ.

And these things write we unto you, that your joy may be full."

Love for Him and an agape love for others will compel you to evangelize. If we love the Lord Jesus, we will do what He commands, and we know that His great mandate is for us to evangelize the world.

It Is A Personal Thing

One of the first lessons that should be learned is that there a need for a personal relationship with God, through Jesus Christ, and the controlling power of the Holy Spirit in your life. God has called and chosen us to be an ambassador, and a reconciler with God, through the power of the Holy Spirit. Nothing will take the place of being occupied fully by the Holy Spirit, and working in complete dependency on the Lord.

Acts 2:4, "And they were all filled with the Holy Ghost, and began to speak with other tongues, as the Spirit gave them utterance."

Ephesians 5:18, "And be not drunk with wine, wherein is excess; but be filled with the Spirit;"

Acts 4:31, "And when they had prayed, the place was shaken where they were assembled together; and they were all filled with the Holy Ghost, and they spake the word of God with boldness."

Evangelism Requires Flexibility

Another lesson that I have learned in evangelizing and will never forget is that there is a need to break from some traditional approaches. There is no substitute for following the leadership of the Holy Spirit. One should totally depend upon the authority of Jesus Christ.

Act 13:2-4, "As they ministered to the Lord, and fasted, the Holy Ghost said, Separate me Barnabas and Saul for the work whereunto I have called them. And when they had fasted and prayed, and laid their hands on them, they sent them away. So they, being sent forth by the Holy Ghost, departed unto Seleucia; and from thence they sailed to Cyprus."

Paul and Barnabas were making, by the leadership of the Holy Spirit, a break from tradition.

If Not You, Then Who?

There were times when I honestly did not know what to do or where to go. Whenever you are not sure, do nothing but pray. When in the valley of decision about your call or evangelistic work, then volunteer.

There are two ways to get into the armed services, by being drafted or to volunteer. Both ways are biblical for the service of the Lord. The more traditional way is waiting until drafted. On the other hand, we find in:

> **Isaiah 6:8, "Also I heard the voice of the Lord, saying, Whom shall I send, and who will go for us? Then said I, here am I; send me."**

Isaiah volunteered for the Lord's service and the Lord took him up on it and said, **"Go and tell this people, hear ye indeed, but understand not; and see ye indeed, but perceive not."**

Whether volunteering or being drafted, we are partners with the Lord, and not, "for" the Lord. If people are to be saved, the Lord must save them, and we along with the lost, must cooperate with the redemptive plan of God through Jesus Christ. **Acts 10:1-48.** Everyone saved can and should evangelize. It is God's will for every Christian or believer, in the Lord Jesus Christ, to evangelize.

Evangelism Requires Preparation

Attending bible school, taking bible classes, or going to seminary for formal training will result in more than words could express.

> **II Timothy 2:15, "Study to show thyself approved unto God, a workman that needeth not to be ashamed, rightly dividing the word of truth."**

> **II Timothy 4:5, "But watch thou in all things, endure afflictions, do the work of an evangelist, make full proof of thy ministry."**

Likewise, physical tools for evangelizing are essential. Knowing this, by the direction of the Lord, I designed a laminated card, outlining the plan of salvation, wrote a witnessing and follow-up booklet, a church brochure, and a simple tract. I used the Christian Life New Testament and acquired a knowledge of the city, as well. I produced evangelistic videos dealing with evangelism and the plan of salvation. I established a radio ministry and a television ministry.

We used any means we could to get out the gospel. We took opportunities to give invitations at funerals, weddings, Wednesday night prayer meetings, and street preaching services. Witnessing and passing out tracts have been very beneficial in our evangelistic efforts. On one occasion, our church passed out more than ten thousand tracts to individuals, who visited the bombing site in the Oklahoma City area at the Alfred P. Murrah Building. No one rejected a tract and none were found on the ground. We sang and prayed with rescue workers, families, and well wishers for twelve days. It was an astonishing thing to witness the mighty hand of God at work.

Following pastoral or evangelistic leadership is very important for productivity in winning the lost to Jesus Christ. As Director of Evangelism for the Northeast Project, a group of concerned ministers, Christians, and community people, we witnessed hundreds coming to the Lord. We accomplished this through marches, street preaching, community picnics, recreation on the streets, food sack giveaways, and a 300 Foot-Soldier Witnessing Team Search Party. At one Praise Rally of the N.E. Project, we witnessed 32 people baptized the same day of the search party. We also had a Memorial March because of the many killed needlessly, in Oklahoma City, Oklahoma. There were about 4,500 Christians and unsaved people from different backgrounds and races. We praise the Lord for fourteen people being baptized after the march.

A systematic way of witnessing or visitation should be taught step-by-step and practiced. We did role playing many times on Wednesday nights and during Sunday evening services. I adopted a particular approach, as an evangelist and used it constantly. I learned and taught a systematic road map or presentation of the plan of salvation for effective evangelizing.

I discovered that we needed a consistent day and time for a thriving visitation or evangelistic program. For more than twenty-six years, I have used Saturdays as a main day to do street preaching, bus ministry, and visitation. Whatever the climate or conditions were, I was determined to preach the word from the street corner. I began my evangelistic ministry preaching at Second and Stiles, where my first convert, was an elderly gentleman in his late sixties, by the name of Willie Mays who accepted Christ. I went from 2nd Street to 4th Street, to 7th and Harrison, to 13th and Walnut, to 23rd Street and Eastern, and other parts of Oklahoma City, preaching the gospel. I decided to go where most would not go, or even consider a pulpit, "the streets". God moved and many lives were changed, and are being changed, by the power of God and the word of God.

A particular location and target group or groups should be considered in evangelistic endeavors. The Street Ministry would take tours throughout the United States over an eight day period in the summer. We would go into different cities to do "the work of the church." We felt Chicago was the toughest city to evangelize. We stayed there four days witnessing and preaching. We saw many saved, although we were never invited into a single house. We also witnessed a shootout at a gas station in Chicago. We tried to intervene by approaching the gang members about Christ. One man went after his gun, and another said, "Reverend, what you are doing is good, but it's no time for that." It was driven home to me that night that everyone would not be reached for the Lord. One of the most receptive cities where we witnessed many coming to the Lord Jesus Christ was in Jackson, Mississippi.

Now before all of this happened, the Lord was gaining my attention to go into full time evangelistic work, He took me to some of the most troublesome spots in our city. God raised a question to me, "If you don't go, then who will?" Although this was a sobering question that gripped my heart initially, I am glad He gave me the courage to say with tears streaming down my face, "Yes Lord, Here am I, send me!"

Jesus Christ went to the lost of Israel. The disciples majored on winning the Jews. Paul went to the Gentiles and throughout the Bible there were target groups that God sent His messengers to win. Dr. Cliet Wilburn profoundly stated, that people would know me as, "the street preacher for street people." His prophecy was fulfilled, and I, by the help of the Lord, spent many hours proclaiming the message of God to the lost from a street corner.

Faith and Evangelism

Pastor H.A. Walker said, "Faith is climbing a house without a ladder." Dr. D.D. Garland stated, "Faith is one step beyond reasoning."

The Hebrew writer wrote,

> **Hebrews 11:1, "Now faith is the substance of things hoped for, the evidence of things not seen."**

Now faith is one step beyond common sense. Faith is hearing God, believing God after you have heard Him, and doing what God says. Faith is saying what God says. Obedience to God is faith in action. Faith is seeing and speaking the unseen reality into existence.

Many things that Father God instructed me to do, at times, seemed irrational to my natural mind. But, rather than live by feelings, or what seemed rational or irrational, I took God at His word. I have obeyed His voice, although at times, some called me insane. I can remember in a prayer meeting, asking the Lord, who will go with me? This humored the Lord, for He began to laugh and said, "Father, Son, and Holy Ghost." Initially, I was alone doing everything with the Lord. When I took tours, it was a wonderful experience, and I learned beyond a doubt that I could totally depend on my Father in Heaven.

We need to remember always:

> **Hebrews 11:6, "But without faith it is impossible to please him: for he that cometh to God must believe that he is, and that he is a rewarder of them that diligently seek him."**

There is no way to please God without completely trusting, depending, and relying on Him in whatever He commands, and anything else is sin.

God will reward any person that will do what He orders. Careful attention and persistent application of God's Word, written or spoken, will be rewarded. I discovered I could not please God without obedience to Him always, in all situations, and under all circumstances. There was forever safety in following His leadership, since I had never been in the streets. I did not know the dangers of working in this arena. I thank God for His wisdom. Sometimes ignorance can be a great blessing. In one ministerial meeting an older preacher sarcastically said, "He is trying to save the world." Years later, I knew that everyone was not complimenting me for doing this type of work. Even my Christian character was challenged. I was accused of doing some unscrupulous things, but I thank the Lord for being my witness. You have to do what you have to do for the Lord. I believe with all my heart, that the Lord is blessing and making us a blessing today because of the work done in the Street Ministry days.

Faith is obeying God and evangelizing the world. For without faith evangelism is futile. Everything I did, required the faith of God. It took faith to be saved, to accept the call of God, and leaving one denomination to go to another. It took faith leaving Kraft Foods as a sales representative to go into full-time evangelistic work.

Faith in God helped us to organize a new church in an area where this type of church had not existed. Faith gave us the strength to build a 1.5 million dollar church building. Faith led me from selling cheese, to proclaiming the wonderful news of God's redemption, to all men everywhere.

Faith led me from city to city, and from state to state witnessing the miraculous power of God through His Word. Faith led me from the sidewalk to a Street Ministry Headquarter, and from having worship services in a nineteen-room house, to a warehouse doing the same. Faith led us from a warehouse to God's house, seating over eleven hundred people. He led us from one van, to vans and buses; from one sanctuary to three; and from owning a lot to owning over fourteen acres of land. Faith led us from mineral rights, to an oil well; from four members, to thousands of members; from supporting a few missionary works, to many; and from a few dollars to millions.

Faith led from one radio broadcast to four broadcasts; from the radio, to over a year and a half on television; from one church, to five extensions; and from one mission to three missions. Faith led from people saying, "Who is that young man preaching on the streets?", to being appointed to the **Governor's Task Force Against Tobacco for Youth.**

Faith led from a few engagements, to many; from one educational degree, to three degrees; and "From Preaching on the Streets to Pastoring in the Pulpit." Faith took me from having a prophet's heart, to a pastor's heart. Faith delivered me from being mistreated by many, to a loving, caring, Church of God.

We have truly come this far by faith, leaning on the Lord. Well, as Rev. Willie Boone, Jr. said, "from just leaning on the Lord to stretching out on Him." Someone has well said "God is Good" but the little old lady said, "He's better than that."

Paul declared in **Galatians 2:20:**

> **"I am crucified with Christ: nevertheless I live; yet not I, but Christ liveth in me: and the life which I now live in the flesh I live by the faith of the Son of God, who loved me, and gave himself for me."**

Without faith, nothing can be done to please God including evangelizing the world. The church can and must evangelize the world, by the faith of God and by faith in God.

Evangelism and Prayer

Prayer is asking and allowing God to talk with you, and to you. **"It Happens After Prayer",** was a statement I heard from the lips of Rev. H.A. Walker. This statement became a vital part of my life and others that God allowed me to influence all over America. I discovered prayer not only changed people, but circumstances and situations. True prayer originates in the heart of God. If prayer does not start and end with God, it is not prayer. We should always ask the Holy Spirit to help us pray.

> **Matthew 7:7-11, "Ask, and it shall be given you; seek, and ye shall find; knock, and it shall be opened unto you: For every one that asketh receiveth; and he that seeketh findeth; and to him that knocketh it shall be opened. Or what man is there of you, whom if his son ask bread, will he give him a stone? Or if he ask a**

> **fish, will he give him a serpent? If ye then, being evil, know how to give good gifts unto your children, how much more shall your Father which is in heaven give good things to them that ask him?"**

It was through prayer that victory came in overcoming sin, Satan, and habits. Through prayer, people are saved, delivered, and healed. Through prayer, Satan is defeated and lives are changed. Through prayer, the worse can become the best, the bad can become the good, the unfaithful, the faithful, the stingy, the givers, the unconcerned, the concerned, and the lost, the found.

> **II Chronicles 14:7, "Therefore he said unto Judah, Let us build these cities, and make about them walls, and towers, gates, and bars, while the land is yet before us; because we have sought the LORD our God, we have sought him, and he hath given us rest on every side. So they built and prospered."**

> **II Chronicles 7:14, "If my people, which are called by name, shall humble themselves, and pray, and seek my face, and turn from their wicked ways; then I hear from heaven, and will forgive their sin, and will heal their land."**

I can remember going to the prayer room at St. James Baptist Church and praying for hours in the beginning of my Christian pilgrimage. Through prayer, God began to unveil His will for my life. After receiving access to the church key, I can recall going to church late at night and taking other brothers praying for hours for God's illumination, revelation, wisdom, inspiration, and understanding. One night, we took my brother Bobby Joe and, he received the Lord.

While praying another night, a member that lived across from the church, called the Pastor to inform him of a break-in at the church. When the Pastor arrived, he found us in a heated prayer meeting. We would start praying after midnight and sometimes pray until two, or four o'clock in the morning. God would give us assignments and directions through these prayer meetings.

This trend eventually led Pastor Parker, and other members and ministers of the church to do the same for several years. We prayed in the dark with all the lights off.

> **St. Luke 6:12 It states, "And it came to pass in those days, that he went out into a mountain to pray, and continued all night in prayer to God."**

Praying, listening, and hearing God became a reality as a young Christian. Through these late night prayer meetings, came sermons, visions, revelations, understanding, and Divine appointments. The Street Ministry, Inc. was born after prayer. I became a full-time salesman, with Kraft Foods after quitting a tobacco company through prayer. In seventy-two years of existence, Kraft Foods had not maintained a full-time African American Salesman, but I was chosen. Through prayer, I discovered the will of God for my full-time evangelistic work. Through prayer, our church was organized.

After prayer, the church began to see tremendous amounts of growth in a short period of time. Missions, extensions, and outreach ministries were established from our core church. Prayer involves talking to God, listening, believing, and obeying the small, clear, majestic voice of Him, through His Spirit.

In I Kings 19:11-12, "And he said, Go forth, and stand upon the mount before the LORD. And, behold, the LORD passed by, and a great and strong wind rent the mountains, and brake in pieces the rocks before the LORD; but the LORD was not in the wind: and after the wind an earthquake; but the LORD was not in the earthquake: And after the earthquake a fire; but the LORD was not in the fire: and after the fire a still small voice."

Do not just pray, and stop. Pray, then stop, and listen to the voice of God. Praying to God mingled with faith yields great results every time. A misconception when praying is that we do all of the talking, asking, interceding, and praising God, however, we do not stop and listen to Him for instructions. God wants to help us pray through His Spirit, and the Spirit of God wants us to know the will of God. When we follow God's leadership success is certain. It is always good to pray for God's will to be done.

I can remember vividly witnessing twice a day, every day, when our church was first organized. It seemed to me that the harder we worked, the less would happen. The Lord showed me, He wanted to do the work. He would work, if we would pray. Our prayers involve God and moves Him to do the work.

Our emphasis changed from always witnessing to praying, "fellowshipping", and worshiping God more. It was amazing to see how God began to save and add believers to His church. We later learned the highest form of prayer is praise. Praise will move God every time. The church in many areas needs to learn, that praise is prayer.

"It Happens After Prayer." Have you tried praying? "Pray about everything, and worry about nothing," a statement from Dr. G. Vernon McGee. Everything we did was turned into a prayer meeting, even telephone conversations. Only God knows the many hurtful, deadly, challenging situations we have been delivered from, through prayer, praise, and thanksgiving. When in trouble, pray your way out. Stop worrying and trying to figure your way out. **"It Happens After Prayer."**

A great deal of emphasis was placed on the importance of our church praying. We witnessed untold miracles through God's Divine intervention and through the power, joy, and responsibility of praying. **"It Happens After Prayer."**

God's people have been delivered, the unsaved, saved, the unchurched, churched, backsliders reclaimed, the believers equipped, land and building purchased, monies received, marriages restored, children reclaimed, people healed, the captive delivered, and many other things have happened, because we embraced the God, who hears and answers prayers.

> **Jeremiah 33:3, "Call unto me, and I will answer thee, and show thee great and mighty things, which thou knowest not."**

We have witnessed well over 300 in prayer meeting in our church. Many times we are the answer to our own prayers. Maybe this is the reason so many Christians are not attending prayer meetings. The failure to hear God and respond to His will produces nothing. We need not forget we are partners with God. The Church needs to know **prayer** and **evangelism** are running partners. You cannot have the one without the other.

> **Do as the Lord Commands in Luke 10:2 "Therefore said he unto them, The harvest truly is great, but the labourers are few: pray ye therefore the Lord of the harvest, that he would send forth labourers into his harvest."**

There is no way to pray for laborers or workers without becoming one yourself. Pray and begin experiencing the mighty hand of God at work. He will work in us, through us, to will and do His good pleasure, if we pray.

> **Hebrews 4:16, "Let us therefore come boldly unto the throne of grace, that we may obtain mercy, and find grace to help in time of need."**

Let us as Believers "go in and keep going in" because, **"It Happens After Prayer."** Don't wait another minute, because, **"It Happens After Prayer."**

Prayer and Evangelism go hand in hand! **Jesus, Lord Jesus, Jesus Got It Going On In Every Christian's Life, If You Let Him.**

Giving and Evangelism

While conducting a revival in Dallas, Texas, at a local church for five days, I had the opportunity to trust God for my daily needs. The Church did not offer me lodging or food the entire week except a meal on the last night after the revival meeting. I had to stay in a small four room house that the Street Ministry rented in Dallas, Texas. There were no utilities in the house due to a lack of funds.

I was surprised while in Oklahoma, God instructed me to take our baby's old mattress with me. As you might guess, I ended up using the mattress as a bed on the floor for sleeping every night. This was done because of a lack of finances for proper accommodations. The Lord also, told me to take some candles which I used for lighting to keep roaches off me in the house. I can remember one night the mosquitos got so bad that I slept in my little orange Vega station wagon. At the end of the revival, I received $22.50 for the entire week.

Before going home, I was waiting to talk to a local pastor about supporting our ministry which he did not, and a young teenage boy hit my car. It had been raining and the streets were slippery. This young man had no insurance coverage therefore, I had to pay a $100 insurance deductible to get my car repaired.

The Lord used heartbreaking and painful encounters such as this one, to deepened my understanding and commitment for the necessity of the Church to teach and practice giving to the work of God. One of the greatest hindrances to evangelizing is a lack of finances.

> **"And how shall they preach, except they be sent?"**
> **Romans 10:15a**

God's plan has not changed concerning financing His program and for evangelizing the world. God's way of financing His program is still through tithes and offerings.

God is always the giver of all things. He is the source of meeting all of our needs. The tithe and the offering should be given as God gives so that there may be substance in God's house, to fulfill the purpose and plan of God.

> **Malachi 3:10, "Bring ye all the tithes into the storehouse, that there may be meat in mine house, and prove me now herewith, saith the LORD of hosts, if I will not open you the windows of heaven, and pour you out a blessing, that there shall not be room enough to receive it."**

The tithe blesses God's house and the offering is a blessing to your house. An outreach ministry needs the people of God to give to meet the needs of the ministry. There were many times in the Street Ministry days that tremendous amounts of financial suffering took place because of a lack of funds for our ministry. It was difficult for most churches to support an untraditional ministry.

I recall my wife asking me, "Why is it, that you give the little back that we receive?" Although my answer was not clear within my own thinking, I replied, "You have to trust me." We trusted the Lord and He made a way.

Many Christians would not and did not support our work financially as a Street Ministry. I did not understand that type of mentality as an evangelist. I know now as a Pastor, that many Christians do not support their own church. This explains why they did not support our ministry.

Many pastors, in the Street Ministry days, told me they could not afford to contribute ten dollars a month to our ministry. Some said that they would and never did. Many revivals and Sunday morning honorariums were less than average, because of Christians who did not know the benefits of giving or lacked the love to do so. My family suffered immensely due to the lack of finances. Many evangelists, missionaries, staff workers, and pastors have and are suffering because of a lack of proper finances in God's house. The church needs to remember and practice the words of our Lord Jesus Christ in:

> **Luke 6:38, "Give, and it shall be given unto you; good measure, pressed down, and shaken together, and running over, shall men give into your bosom. For with the same measure that ye mete withal it shall be measured to you again."**

And according to Paul in:

> **Ephesians 6:8, "Knowing that whatsoever good thing any man doeth, the same shall he receive of the Lord, whether he be bond or free."**

And in:

> **Philippians 4:16,17,19, "For even in Thessaloncia ye sent once and again unto my necessity. Not because I desire a gift: but I desire fruit that may abound to your account. But my God shall supply all your need according to his riches in glory by Christ Jesus."**

I learned that God is more than able to meet the needs of His people despite the situations, or circumstances. Even when we had little support for our Street Ministry, God met the needs. It was not a cake walk however, through the grace, mercy, love, and help of God, I continued four and a half years as a full-time Evangelist and Street Preacher.

The experiences made me a better Pastor-Teacher. I learned and taught the importance of teaching and practicing giving. As a Pastor, I made a promise to God not to mistreat any man of God that the Father sent, or allowed to help His Church in the Lord's work.

> **Matthew 25:40, "And the King shall answer and say unto them, Verily I say unto you, Inasmuch as ye have done it unto one of the least of these my brethren, ye have done it unto me."**

I saw and understood the gravity of supporting other God called works. God showed me the responsibility of every church ministry meeting needs outside of itself. We began teaching the church the necessity of biblical economical support for God's work within and without. We are to be witnesses in Jerusalem, and in all Judaea, and in Samaria, and unto the uttermost part of the earth.

As the newly called Pastor of the Del City Missionary Baptist Church, my starting salary was twenty-five dollars a week as the church grew, our finances increased, and so did my salary. Our first missionary support came through the church tithing to our mission account and making faith promises. Our background scriptures for faith promises are found in:

> **I Samuel 1:11; 19B, 20, "And she vowed a vow, and said, O LORD of hosts, if thou wilt indeed look on the affliction of thine handmaid, and remember me, and not forget thine handmaid, but wilt give unto thine handmaid a man child, then I will give him unto the LORD all the days of his life, and there shall no razor come upon his head. . . and the LORD remembered her. Wherefore it came to pass, when the time was come about after Hannah had conceived, that she bare a son, and called his name Samuel, saying, Because I have asked him of the LORD."**

Our newly organized church gave twenty-four hundred dollars to missionary works outside ourselves during the first six months. This was the beginning of God making and giving us the grace to give. Due to the rapid growth of the church, needs were springing up everywhere. God gave us the spirit, the fortitude, and the perseverance to meet our needs, but this was not done without opposition from the Devil.

I thank God for the courage He gave us to resist the wiles of Satan, and the power to stand on the Word of God. Through teaching the Word of God on giving, our tithes, offerings, and faith promise increased. Favorable results come through preaching and teaching on any given subject.

Each year for five years, our monies and support continued to be strong, even though we were spreading and starting new extension works from the Core Church. We purchased vehicles for transportation, bought land, buildings, built a new educational wing and sanctuary on some newly acquired properties at 4621 N.E. 23rd Street in Oklahoma City.

In the latter part of 1985, it seemed like the roof was caving in on our church. People began to leave for various reasons and the economical situations in Oklahoma took a turn for the worse with the oil crash. After going through several bond programs, the Lord began elevating us again in the early nineties. Faithfulness is a valuable weapon in the Holy Spirit if you will not give up and take off.

God takes everything that happens to us as Christians, good or bad, and works these things out for our ultimate success. Paul wrote in:

> **Romans 8:28, "And we know that all things work together for good to them that love God, to them who are the called according to his purpose."**

So we plainly see, that nothing bad can happen to a Christian, and there is no such thing, as a child of God having bad luck.

> **Psalms 30:5B, ". . .weeping may endure for a night, but joy cometh in the morning."**

As a young preacher, I always thought that things could only get better, never worse. Every pastor should count the cost and pray earnestly for Divine directions before doing anything for, and with God's people. Even the people of God will let you down, but praises be to God, the Father will not.

Sometimes Satan's temptation becomes God's test. Four years ago, I was challenged by a young preacher to start teaching our people about giving, in particular, sowing and reaping. At first, I was offended. However, I discovered that he was only being used by God, to help me to look deeper into the grace of giving.

God brought us through the stages of paying tithes, offerings, and faith promise giving. We then started giving, as some would say, "until it hurt" or "sacrificially". Eventually, we grew in our giving, sowing, reaping, and expecting to see, what we gave multiplied back. The Lord promised if we would give that he would give back to us good measure, pressed down, shaken together, and running over. God has led us occasionally, to send a love offering to another needful ministry even when we were in dire need. As we obeyed the leadership of the Holy Spirit, the Lord met our need no matter how great.

In these days of difficulties and selfishness, teaching biblical economics as a means necessary for worldwide evangelization, is extremely hard, nevertheless, it is imperative. It takes a committed, dedicated, consecrated man of God, to meet the challenges of today's churches and ministries.

It takes a true man of God, not to listen to all the voices on broadway, but to hear and obey God. God's people would do better usually if they knew better. God is going to hold the overseers accountable for what they do not do, as well as, what they do.

The average believer has not been delivered in the area of giving. Some preachers declare, "Do as I say, and not as I do." God cannot elevate a church any higher, than its leader. If a church has an insensitive, survival conscience leader, then the church will be no better.

The subject of giving has been ignored for fear of losing members. Without proper finances, the church cannot accomplish great things. There is a growing need for the church to take her biblical precedent in this area of supporting and providing for God's work and God's people. Some churches are missionary inclined in their financial support for missionary work, but when it comes to helping one another financially in the local church, they are cold hearted. Some are church supportive but not missionary supportive. There has to be a balance and with the help of the Holy Spirit, the church must do both. We would not have made it through our great times of financial turbulence, without the teachings of the Holy Spirit and having Spirit-led people. As a church, we were propelled into a period of believing God as a ministry, or dying as a failure.

Suffering produces patience, patience yields experience, and experience makes for mature believers that are givers. I thank God for a giving church at 4621 N.E. 23rd in Oklahoma City, Oklahoma.

Our hardships became blessings for others. We as a church discovered that God, through Jesus Christ, had blessed us to be a blessing. Any ministry or church should not only be able to sustain itself but should also help others to walk in the will of God. This outreach support should not come with hidden agendas from the church giving support. God wants every church to reach out by the command of the Spirit, in love, reaching the saved and the lost, with financial help that will make an eternal difference.

> **Paul wrote in Philippians 4:15-17, "Now ye Philippians know also, that in the beginning of the gospel, when I departed from Macedonia, no church communicated with me as concerning giving and receiving, but ye only. For even in Thessalonica ye sent once and again unto my necessity. Not because I desire a gift: but I desire fruit that may abound to your account."**

Giving always benefits the receiver, and the giver. God receives thanks, praise, and glory, when we give from our hearts . The receiver's need is met with thanksgiving. The Lord has given us a ministry of meeting the needs of our members, missionaries, and other churches. We have a food closet, a very costly bus ministry, a youth program, and other outreach endeavors. When times get hard, there is always a tendency to retreat and play it safe. When in actuality, we should obey God. Obedience to God always produces blessings and deliverance. Blessed ministries should always be a blessing to the struggling. How God longs for us to help one another. There have been times I have prayed that God's people would just see.

> **I John 3:17, "But whoso hath this world's good, and seeth his brother have need, and shutteth up his bowels of compassion from him, how dwelleth the love of God in him?"**

Rather than seeing and meeting the needs of God's people, Christians have a tendency to sneer. For this great sin, we will answer to God. You see, with God's people possessing the Holy Spirit, we have been given the ability to see needs. There is no need for the people of God to ask. I thank God, through our woes, we had one Christian brother, outside our church to offer help, and one who actually helped us financially. May the Lord help us to see our brother's needs and to meet them. May the Lord help us to hear the voice of God when it comes to giving. Too few, hear God when it comes to giving outside of their personal agendas.

Our church motto is, "Meeting human needs because God cares." Could it be, that is why, it is so easy for a church to stay in the comfort of its four walls, and not evangelize, because of the financial cost? As Rev. Louis Parker would say, "We don't have it made." At Christian

Life, we have learned the joy of sharing with God's people. God loves a happy giver, and a happy giver loves God and God's people.

When there is a genuine need of the church or a worthy cause, I have discovered that God's people will always find a way to give. They will find a way to do the things needed and necessary to sustain the integrity of God. Love will always cost, just like it cost God, in the giving of His Son's life, that we may live eternally, in mercy and grace. Love was not free to God and we are not greater than He. Salvation is free to us, but it had a tremendous cost to God. The Son of God purchased us with His very blood.

Some of God's people fail to give all of the tithe and the offering. They only go, "piece of the way", in giving an acceptable offering, in the sight of God. They do that which is pleasing, in their own eyes. It seems like, Mr. George Washington (the dollar) is the only one worthy of giving to God, or His people. This has caused the church to remain on first base for the last thirty years or more.

It's almost like God's people pray about everything except what to give in the offering plate. Only a Holy Spirit directed Church can meet the vast needs of a contemporary society where there is always a need to give. For years, I believed without scriptural validation that giving to God or man should have been done without **expecting** anything but joy and gratitude for the gift.

After many years of giving, God has shown me that God's people have been giving their offerings the wrong way. We should always give, as God gave, expecting a return from the gift.

> **In John 3:16 "For God so loved the world, that he gave his only begotten Son, that whosoever believeth in him should not perish, but have everlasting life."**

God gave His Son expecting this seed to produce many sons. The principle of giving to get, is from the heart of God. Jesus declared in.....

> **Luke 6:38 "Give, and it shall be given unto you; good measure, pressed down, and shaken together, and running over, shall men give into your bosom. For with the same measure that ye mete withal it shall be measured to you again."**

> **Paul wrote in Galatians 6:7 "Be not deceived; God is not mocked: for whatsoever a man soweth, that shall he also reap."**

And again, Paul wrote in:

> **II Corinthians 9:6 "But this I say, He which soweth sparingly shall reap also sparingly; and he which soweth bountifully shall reap also bountifully."**

These scriptures point out the benefit of giving to receive. There is no greater soil to give to, than your church, your pastor, a true man of God, a Christian, or a biblical ministry. There is no greater reason for giving, than to evangelize the world, to Jesus Christ our Lord. When we give God is glorified, the lost is saved, and the believer is edified and made a blessing.

There is a word of warning to the wise. Some men of God and church leaders move too fast, and want too much, too soon. This will cause a financial strain on the immature Christians in the church. The loss of some of the membership will be inevitable. A negative reputation will develop, because of the necessity to mention the need for more money. It is good to be very cautious in this area of the church's ministry. There is also a tendency with a new thriving ministry to want more than is necessary. If they yield to this type of temptation, it will produce financial problems that can become overwhelming. Many people have deserted God's will for their lives, because of financial pressures in the house of God. Be wise enough to avoid this type of situation. On the other hand, some churches have been on first base for the last thirty years or more. They are being what they call moderate, but the truth of the matter is, they have little faith and wrong priorities. This type of mentality and action, will stagnate the church for years to come. You can have what you want, if you wait but do not wait too long, it can become a sin. Always remember that God, our Father is in complete control. He will see you through no matter what the circumstance, if you trust Him. We must know, **evangelism** and **giving** go hand and hand.

Some Christians have been giving without acknowledgment of God's Lordship, without expecting a return, and without a purpose. Everything we do should be done in Jesus Christ's Name, by His Authority, in the power of the Holy Spirit. God wants all His people to give expecting what they have given, to be multiplied back.

This great truth learned and practiced, launched our church into a new vitality for giving and supporting the work of the Lord. Every pastor should teach the People of God the advantage of giving. When people learn the benefits of doing business with God, they will become givers.

Do not forget there will be no worldwide evangelism without proper finances. You never, ever lose, by giving to the Lord's work.

Christian Life Missionary Baptist Church Extension in Madrid, Spain.

Christian Life Missionary Baptist Church Extension in Tulsa, Oklahoma.

LivingWord Missionary Baptist Church , the first Mission that developed into a Independent Church.

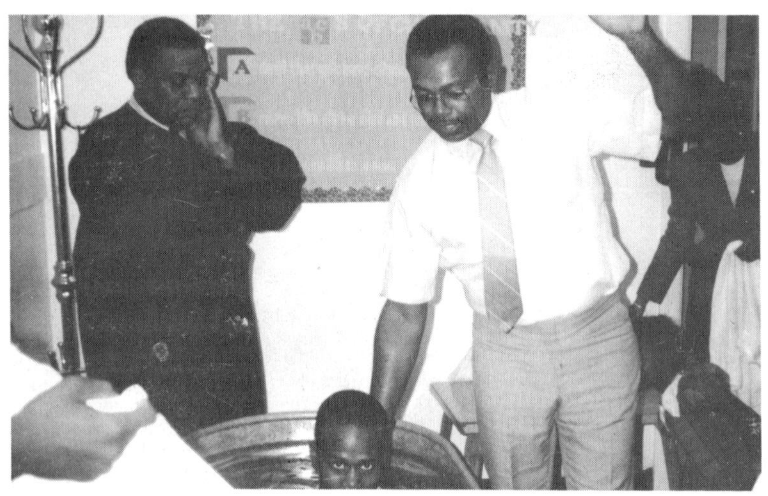

Pastor Jacobs observing Pastor James R. Alston at Christian Life Missionary Baptist Church Extension in Goldsboro, North Carolina.

Christian Life Missionary Baptist Church Northwest Mission in Oklahoma City, Oklahoma.

Chapter Five
Some Methodologies For Evangelism

- People will be untruthful.

  Acts 5:3, "But Peter said, Ananias, why hath Satan filled thine heart to lie to the Holy Ghost, ... "

- When someone tells you that they will come the next Sunday . . . that means they are not coming at all, or they will come when you least expect them.

  Luke 14:18a, "And they all with one consent began to make excuse."

- When people start crying or become very emotional, watch out and pray hard.

  I Peter 4:7 "But the end of all things is at hand: be ye therefore sober, and watch unto prayer."

- Do not try to witness to a large group of people. Isolate them and get one on one. New witnessing teams might start by witnessing to teens or passing out tracts.

  Matthew 10:16 "Behold, I send you forth as sheep in the midst of wolves: be ye therefore wise as serpents, and harmless as doves."

- A good test of a person receiving the Lord Jesus Christ is:

  I John 4:1-3 "Beloved, believe not every spirit, but try the spirits whether they are of God: because many false prophets are gone out into the world. Hereby

know ye the Spirit of God: Every spirit that confesseth that Jesus Christ is come in the flesh is of God: And every spirit that confesseth not that Jesus Christ is come in the flesh is not of God: and this is that spirit of antichrist, whereof ye have heard that it should come; and even now already is it in the world."

- When people close the door on you, they are closing the door on Jesus Christ, not you. Do not take it personally and be offended.

Matthew 10:14 "And whosoever shall not receive you, nor hear your words, when ye depart out of that house or city, shake off the dust of your feet."

John 15:20, "Remember the word that I said unto you, The servant is not greater than his lord. If they have persecuted me, they will also persecute you; if they have kept my saying, they will keep yours also."

- Always go witnessing in two(s) or more.
- Males should witness to males and females should witness to females. In heavily crime areas, a male-female partnership may be better.

Luke 14:23 "And the lord said unto the servant, Go out into the highways and hedges, and compel them to come in, that my house may be filled."

- Some people have been saved, but not baptized. Water baptism comes after conversion, not before.

Mark 16:16, "He that believeth and is baptized shall be saved; but he that believeth not shall be damned."

- Be alert to have all witnessing tools, not your big white or black family Bible, but a New Testament, a pen, witnessing cards, tracts, and a witnessing notebook.

Ephesians 5:16, "Redeeming the time, because the days are evil."

- Do not let fear stop you from going. God does not give this spirit, but guess who does?

II Timothy 1:7 "For God hath not given us the spirit of fear; but of power, and of love, and of a sound mind."

- Evangelism can take place wherever you are.

  - Gas Stations
  - Stores
  - Jobs
  - Home
  - Street Corners
  - Schools
  - Parks
  - Divine Appointments

Mark 16:15 "And he said unto them, Go ye into all the world, and preach the gospel to every creature."

- When street preaching, go where the people are heavily populated, usually on a busy, highly visible, street corner. There is also safety in doing it this way. A place where people can stop, park, and listen to the message. A highly populated neighborhood is also a good place to set up and preach.

Matthew 5:1 "And seeing the multitudes, he went up into a mountain: and when he was set, his disciples came unto him:"

- I can remember preaching in Jackson, Mississippi in a black neighborhood, and to my amazement, the entire block responded to the invitation to pray and many accepted Christ. I preferred preaching on the streets in a neighborhood, rather than downtown, or in a business section. Using a microphone in the neighborhood is most likely not to receive resistance when preaching. Proper equipment is a must. A microphone and cord, a ten inch horn, an amplifier, and a working car cigarette lighter for street preaching is necessary. You may want to get a microphone permit from the proper authority. But always know that Jesus Christ is the authority of proclamation.

- Learn to sing and "tune," if you plan to be a street preacher. Getting and keeping a person's attention is truly the work of the Holy Spirit. The proper attire is to wear a suit, dress shirt, and tie for most occasions. Even the women should be well-groomed. It is already difficult enough just being on the streets.

> **Proverbs 11:30 "The fruit of the righteous is a tree of life; and he that winneth souls is wise."**

- Watch for people sitting in their cars, standing in their doorways, or just sitting and listening when preaching on the streets. God has drawn these people by His Spirit and prepared their hearts for salvation. You should deal with them in a personal manner. It is always good to have a partner to help in this kind of situation.

> **Acts 1:8 "But ye shall receive power, after that the Holy Ghost is come upon you: and ye shall be witnesses unto me both in Jerusalem, and in all Judaea, and in Samaria, and unto the uttermost part of the earth."**

- Report back to your evangelistic leader or pastor.

Luke 10:17 "And the seventy returned again with joy, saying, Lord, even the devils are subject unto us through thy name."

Acts 14:27 "And when they were come, and had gathered the church together, they rehearsed all that God had done with them, and how he had opened the door of faith unto the Gentiles."

- Do not pass the harvest looking for a person to win.

Luke 10:2 "Therefore said he unto them, The harvest truly is great, but the labourers are few: pray ye therefore the Lord of the harvest, that he would send forth labourers into his harvest."

- Many times your blessings are in your own backyard.

St. John 4:35 "Say not ye, There are yet four months, and then cometh harvest? behold, I say unto you, Lift up your eyes, and look on the fields; for they are white already to harvest." (your friends, family, and relationships)

- When scouting for territory, or a new area to work in a bus ministry look for signs of children living in that area such as: no grass, toys in the yard, certain style of automobile in the driveway. Younger couples usually drive a certain type of car, truck, or van. Territorial responsibilities should be given to each witnessing or visitation team. The more familiar a witnessing team is with a particular area, the better job they will be able to do.

Matthew 7:8b "and he that seeketh findeth;....."

- Remember to get on common ground. Talk about the weather, plants, the house, the family, sports, etc., when beginning a witnessing session.

  St. John 4:7 "There cometh a woman of Samaria to draw water: Jesus saith unto her, Give me to drink."

- Be sure to introduce yourself and give the name of your church, clearly and plainly, to eliminate any notion that you are a member of a cult.

  Luke 10:5-6 "And into whatsoever house ye enter, first say, Peace be to this house. And if the son of peace be there, your peace shall rest upon it: if not, it shall turn to you again . "

- Leave a church brochure or tract with your church's name, address, phone number, and some information about your church. Every church should have a God given church logo.

  Mark 8:29 "And he saith unto them, But whom say ye that I am? And Peter answereth and saith unto him, Thou art the Christ."

- Never put a tract or brochure in a mailbox. The church brochure should be motivational and informational.
- When witnessing with a **partner**, determine who will be the **silent partner**. The **silent partner** prays and keeps order, for an atmosphere of telling the good news.
- Nothing done for the Lord is by chance or in vain.

  I Corinthians. 15:58 "Therefore, my beloved brethren, be ye stedfast, unmovable, always abounding in the work of the Lord, forasmuch as ye know that your labour is not in vain in the Lord."

- The last house, the last hour, the last person, or the last place usually makes the experience, in the Lord, worth it all.

  Galatians 6:9 "And let us not be weary in well doing: for in due season we shall reap, if we faint not."

- Things done with the wrong motives are a waste of time and energy.

  Acts 8:18,19, "And when Simon saw that through laying on of the apostles' hands the Holy Ghost was given, he offered them money, Saying, Give me also this power, that on whomsoever I lay hands, he may receive the Holy Ghost."

  Matthew 6:5 "And when thou prayest, thou shalt not be as the hypocrites are: for they love to pray standing in the synagogues and in the corners of the streets, that they may be seen of men. Verily I say unto you, They have their reward."

  Psalms 127:1 "Except the Lord build the house, they labour in vain that build it: except the Lord keep the city, the watchman waketh but in vain."

- Evangelistic expository preaching is a requirement, if people are to be brought to the Lord.

  Mark 1:14,15 "Now after that John was put in prison, Jesus came into Galilee, preaching the gospel of the kingdom of God, And saying, The time is fulfilled, and the kingdom of God is at hand: repent ye, and believe the gospel."

- An invitation to repent and believe on the Lord Jesus Christ should always be given at every event, including family reunions. This invitational appeal and the method used should be adapted to each occasion.

Matthew 11:28 "Come unto me, all ye that labour and are heavy laden, and I will give you rest."

- How redundantly sad it is to experience great singing and great preaching in city-wide revival services, simultaneous revival services, state-wide revival services, evangelistic conference services, mass inspirational services, and even at convention services, but when an invitation is extended to the lost, not one lost person "comes" for salvation. This happens mainly because there are no unsaved people present in these services to come. The church has to plan, prepare, and bring the unsaved or unchurched into the house of God and the service of God, by evangelizing to see them "come" for salvation. At the invitation in all these types of services, the lost and unchurched should be coming to the Lord Jesus Christ.
- People who are lost will receive prayer when they will not receive the Lord Jesus Christ. Pray for the Holy Spirit to convict the person of sin, righteousness, and judgment. Now watch and see the working power of God.

Prayer Meeting held outside at 23rd and Martin Luther King for those who had been victimized by the bombing in Oklahoma City.

The Christian Life Missionary Baptist Church Choir is singing to the bystanders and praying for the rescue workers at the Alfred P. Murrah Federal Building site, in Oklahoma City.

Taking Back Our City through the Power of Prayer and Proclamation.

Dr. Jacobs, Director of Evangelism for the Northeast Project leads the community in "Taking Back Our City."

Chapter Six
Follow-Up In Evangelism

Biblical follow-up will stop converts from going out the back door. How disappointing it is for new converts to unite with the church get baptized and then never return to the church again. Biblical follow-up is a vital part of Biblical evangelism. Without proper follow-up, there can never be New Testament Evangelism.

My Definition of Biblical Follow-up

The compassionate caring for God's new people, in the power of the Holy Spirit, so that they may continue to follow Jesus Christ as Lord, and develop into learning, teaching, witnessing, and training Christians.

The Essentials of Biblical Follow-Up

Some responsibilities of follow-up are to: love, feed, protect, train, set right, restore, and reinstate. We need to deal with new converts like loving parents treat their children.

Paul believed that personal contact and personal time with new believers were most effective in building Christ in their lives. If possible, a special class and a trained person, should be a part of every new convert's life. New members' classes in every department is imperative. The first twenty-four hours are the most important, in every new Christian's life.

The authority of Biblical follow-up is the Lord Jesus Christ. He knew that His people would go various places and while going, He wanted them to make disciples. Jesus Christ commands us in **Matthew 28: 19-20 to, "Go ye therefore, and teach all nations, baptizing them in the name of the Father, and of the Son, and of the Holy Ghost: Teaching them to observe all things whatsoever I have commanded you: and, lo, I am with you alway, even unto the end of the world. Amen."**

The great mandate reveals to us the mission of every church, which is to witness to the lost, to teach and train the saved. The purpose for Biblical follow-up is to bring into maturity God's new race so they can do the work of the ministry of Jesus Christ and possess doctrinal stability. Jesus Christ wanted the disciples to teach others how to live, as He taught them to develop into maturing, victorious disciples, doing the will of God the Father.

> **Ephesians 4:11-16, "And he gave some, apostles; and some, prophets; and some, evangelists; and some, pastors and teachers;"**
>
> **"For the perfecting of the saints, for the work of the ministry, for the edifying of the body of Christ: Till we all come in the unity of the faith, and of the knowledge of the Son of God, unto a perfect man, unto the measure of the stature of the fullness of Christ:"**
>
> **"That we henceforth be no more children, tossed to and fro, and carried about with every wind of doctrine, by the sleight of men, and cunning craftiness, whereby they lie in wait to deceive;"**
>
> **"But speaking the truth in love, may grow up into him in all things, which is the head, even Christ: From whom the whole body fitly joined together and**

> **compacted by that which every joint supplieth, according to the effectual working in the measure of every part, maketh increase of the body unto the edifying of itself in love."**

Beyond the five fold gifts of the New Testament church, we must mature new converts in a spiritual and practical manner. The process of follow-up is accomplished through edifying, caring, protecting, worshipping, and "fellowshipping" with God's new people.

The method used in biblical follow-up is through teaching and training God's new family. An important factor in follow-up is to make sure that the converts have a genuine born again experience. Many have "Churchanity", or religion, but not "Christ in them, the Hope of Glory." The truly saved continues to walk with Christ by the power of the Holy Spirit and the Word of God living in them.

The saved will follow the Lord Jesus Christ in baptism. They are teachable and trainable. Some people do not, and will not, do any better because they are not saved. Many church people need to have a personal relationship, with the Living Christ, indwelt by the Holy Spirit to live the Life of Christ.

> **According to Acts 2:41-42, "Then they that gladly received his word were baptized: and the same day there were added unto them about three thousand souls."**
>
> **And they continued steadfastly in the apostles' doctrine and fellowship, and in breaking of bread, and in prayers."**

I Peter 2:2-3, "As newborn babes, desire the sincere milk of the word, that ye may grow thereby: If so be ye have tasted that the Lord is gracious."

It is imperative that we baptize newborn Christians the same day if possible, and not wait for the traditional first Sunday. In the New Testament, when people came to the Lord Jesus Christ, they were baptized immediately.

At Christian Life, we keep water in our baptistry so that when the opportunity presents itself, we are ready to do it God's way. We all need to remember the following scriptures, no matter which denomination we are.

Ephesians 4:4-6, "There is one body, and one Spirit, even as ye are called in one hope of your calling; One Lord, one faith, one baptism, One God and Father of all, who is above all and through all, and in you all."

The New Testament method of biblical follow-up is intercessory prayer. This is a very effective method. "**It Happens after Prayer**," and we should pray with them and for them. The Lord Jesus and Paul made this a practice.

John 17;9; 15,17,20, "I pray for them: I pray not for the world, but for them which thou hast given me; for they are thine.

I pray not that thou shouldest take them out of the world, but that thou shouldest keep them from the evil.

Sanctify them through thy truth: thy word is truth. Neither pray I for these alone, but for them also which shall believe on me through their word;"

Philippians 1:9-10, "And this I pray, that your love may abound yet more and more in knowledge and in

all judgement; That ye may approve things that are excellent; that ye may be sincere and without offence till the day of Christ;"

Another method of biblical follow-up is personal contact, to guide the Christian into becoming a faithful witness.

I Thessalonians 3:10, "Night and day praying exceedingly that we might see your face, and might perfect that which is lacking in your faith?"

Acts 22:15, "For thou shalt be his witness unto all men of what thou hast seen and heard."

Acts 15:36, "And some days after Paul said unto Barnabas, Let us go again and visit our brethren in every city where we have preached the word of the Lord, and see how they do."

Galatians 5:16, "This I say then, Walk in the Spirit, and ye shall not fulfill the lust of the flesh."

Sending a substitute is another means of follow-up.

Philippians 2:19-24, "But I trust in the Lord Jesus to send Timothy shortly unto you, that I also may be of good comfort, when I know your state."

"For I have no man likeminded, who will naturally care for your state."

"For all seek their own, not the things which are Jesus Christ's.

But ye know the proof of him, that, as a son with the father, he hath served with me in the gospel.

Him therefore I hope to send presently, so soon as I shall see how it will go with me.

But I trust in the Lord that I also myself shall come shortly."

1 Thessalonians 2:17, "But we, brethren, being taken from you for a short time in presence, not in heart, endeavored the more abundantly to see your face with great desire."

II Timothy 2:2, "And the things that thou hast heard of me among many witnesses, the same commit thou to faithful men, who shall be able to teach others also."

At our church, we have used preachers, deacons, Sunday School teachers, group leaders, staff members and other respected leaders to personally perform the duties of follow-up. Another New Testament way of follow-up is to write letters to the new converts.

Galatians 6:11, "Ye see how large a letter I have written unto you with mine own hand."

I John 2;1, "My little children, these things write I unto you, that ye sin not. And if any man sin, we have an advocate with the Father, Jesus Christ the righteous:"

According to the New Testament, it is as sinful not to teach and train new converts, as it is not to baptize them. The church today typically is long on preaching, short on teaching, and almost without any training especially in spiritual matters. Christianity is practical in every aspect of life.

The Christian Life New Testament published by Thomas Nelson has been a great help. It will help in assisting God's new race of people, to grow in the grace and knowledge of our Lord Jesus Christ. It will be effective because of the fifteen master outlines, by Porter Barrington.

> **II Peter 3:18, "But grow in grace, and in the knowledge of our Lord and Saviour Jesus Christ. To him be glory both now and forever. Amen."**

Spiritual maturity is connected with spiritual knowledge and understanding of the Word of God.

> **Romans 10:17, "So then faith cometh by hearing, and hearing by the word of God."**

Faith always comes from understanding the truth.

Biblical follow-up will close the "back door" in relationship to members uniting and leaving the church. As the church goes and makes disciples with a real relationship with the Lord Jesus and through the authority of Jesus Christ, the back door will be closed. Your objective is to make disciples that will display the righteous character of our Lord and Savior, Jesus Christ. You will need to prepare them to suffer for Him, and they will become stable and endure to the end. They will work while it is day looking for the "soon return" of our Lord and Savior, Jesus Christ. The Lord Jesus Christ commands us to declare this statement, "Even as I have said, that I Am coming, I Am coming soon." A man who makes a disciple makes a learner, in which thousands may come to Jesus Christ.

The Pastor's Responsibility in Follow-up

In **Jeremiah 3:15**, we have a promise from Almighty God that He will give pastors after his own heart. It is imperative that every church possess a true man of God, if you please, a New Testament pastor.

A pastor's chief responsibility is to feed the flock so that they can grow, and render protection from wolves in sheep clothing. They are to give serious time to praying, preaching, teaching, and training the community of faith, or believers in the Lord Jesus Christ. I cannot emphasize too strongly, that the key to a church acquiring and maintaining a healthy spiritual climate lies in the leadership of the pastor doing his work in the Spirit. A pastor engaging in worldliness, carnality, and compromising will not cut the cake, or get the job done.

> **Ephesians 5:18, "And be not drunk with wine, wherein is excess; but be filled with the Spirit:"**
>
> **Romans 8:5-9, 14, "For they that are after the flesh do mind the things of the flesh; but they that are after the Spirit the things of the Spirit."**
>
> **"For to be carnally minded is death; but to be spiritually minded is life and peace."**
>
> **Because the carnal mind is enmity against God: for it is not subject to the law of God, neither indeed can be.**
>
> **"So then they that are in the flesh cannot please God."**
>
> **"But ye are not in the flesh, but in the Spirit, if so be that the Spirit of God dwell in you, Now if any man have not the Spirit of Christ, he is none of his."**

"For as many as are led by the Spirit of God, they are the sons of God."

Acts 20:20, 21, "And how I kept back nothing that was profitable unto you, but have shewed you, and have taught you publicly, and from house to house,

Testifying both to the Jews, and also to the Greeks, repentance toward God, and faith toward our Lord Jesus Christ."

Acts 20;28-29, "Take heed therefore unto yourselves, and to all the flock, over the which the Holy Ghost hath made you overseers, to feed the church of God, which he hath purchased with his own blood.

"For I know this, that after my departing shall grievous wolves enter in among you, not sparing the flock."

First, a pastor must discover the value of one true believer. He must begin with individuals forming cell groups, teaching and training them according to I **Thessalonians 1: 5-9** and **Ephesians 4:11-16.** A pastor must not do the work which the believers are called to do alone. He can only help assist and mentor in the work. He must not be guilty of robbing the believers of their privileges and responsibilities. It is necessary, that he contends for the performance and the work of the church which is to evangelize.

How sad it is for a pastor not to encourage evangelism because of an already full house. God wants the church, even the local church, to reach the world in which His Son died. When your house, or the house of God is full, help fill another house, by continuously working in the field.

Acts 1:8, "But ye shall receive power, after that the Holy Ghost is come upon you: and ye shall be witnesses unto me both in Jerusalem, and in all Judea, and in Samaria, and unto the uttermost part of the earth."

I Thessalonians 1:5-9, "For our gospel came not unto you in word only, but also in power, and in the Holy Ghost, and in much assurance; as ye know what manner of men we were among you for your sake.

And ye became followers of us, and of the Lord, having received the word in much affliction, with joy of the Holy Ghost:

So that ye were examples to all that believe in Macedonia and Achaia.

For from you sounded out the word of the Lord not only in Macedonia and Achaia, but also in every place your faith to God-ward is spread abroad; so that we need not to speak anything.

For they themselves show of us what manner of entering in we had unto you, and how ye turned to God from idols to serve the living and true God;"

The work of the church should be done by believers, but taught by the pastor. It is the task of the pastor to equip the believers through Bible centered preaching, teaching, training and edifying the believers to enhance the work of the church.

Pastors, do your work and believe me, the back door will close. Our task as pastors is to teach and train other believers, to follow the Lord Jesus Christ so that He may teach them to become fishermen and disciple makers.

Ananias taught Paul, Paul taught Timothy, Timothy taught other faithful men, and the faithful men taught others.

There is a famine in the land for real men of God. Jesus Christ was preoccupied with His Father's Word, work, and will. If we are to please God, we must do the same, and do biblical follow-up. **Let discipleship continue.**

Evangelist Jacobs in a red light district preaching hard against sin.

Pastor W.B. Parker and others preaching on 23rd & Eastern during a simultaneous revival.

Open Air Revival.

Pastor Jacobs leads a Memorial March for five women that were killed in a local community.

Chapter Seven
Evangelistic Materials

COUNSELING PROCEDURES

1. **Write the <u>name only</u> on the decision card.**

   (Refer to it as you counsel to be more personal.)

2. ***Determine <u>the need</u>.*** *(Rely on the Holy Spirit.)*
   Ask: ***What did you have in mind when you came forward?***

3. **<u>Meet</u> the need.** *(Use an opened Bible.)*

   <u>A First Time Commitment to Christ:</u>

   *Refer to the plan of salvation laminated card.

   <u>Assurance of Salvation Scriptures</u>

   *Acts 16:30-31

   *Romans 10:9

   *I John 4:1-3

Restoration to the Christian Fellowship

Ask: How do you know you are saved?

*Assurance of Salvation - St. John 3:16-18

*The cause of being out of fellowship- I Peter 3:12

*The need for forgiveness - I John 1:9

*Walk in the Spirit - Romans 8:1-4

*Set a time for prayer - Matthew 26:41

*A time to read and study the Bible - Acts 17:11

*Fellowship with other believers often - Hebrews 10:25

Transfer Membership

*Assurance of Salvation

*Ask: **How do you know you are saved?***

Counselors should give testimonies of what the church means to them. Stress the importance of: daily bible study, prayer time, and faithful church attendance.

If the counselor cannot meet the needs of the person, refer them to the director of follow- up or the pastor. Do not hesitate to seek help.

4. **Finish filling out the decision card completely.**

   *Print

   *Double check information for accuracy

   *Give the card to the Follow-up Director.

5. **Give and explain the Christian survival material, Church Brochure, or other materials designated by the Church.**

   *Emphasize studying the Word of God

   *Emphasize prayer, fellowship, involvement, and faithfulness

6. **Counselor should take a picture with the new member.**

7. **Bring the new member back and present them to the church. Introduce them to the Education Director and the New Member's Teacher or Group Leader.**

8. **If they need to be baptized, escort them to the baptismal committee.**

   A. Water should be prepared

   B. Clothing for baptizing is needed

   C. Pastor or designee should baptize

   D. Clerk gives a baptism certificate

Suggested Revival Preparation Procedures

I. **Organizational preparation** - The preparation for reaching prospects includes the people in the church being prepared for the presence of God in obedience. They must seek to have Him manifest Himself in the revival. They must praise Him, obey Him, and expect Him.

A. All auxiliaries must have a list of prospects for whom they are responsible.

B. Ask members to give names and addresses of neighbors, friends, and relatives that are unsaved and unchurched for follow-up prospects.

C. Cultivate prospects and use concentric circles.

(This is praying for prospects)

D. Ask members to provide addresses of those people that have recently moved into their neighborhoods.

E. Encourage people to visit, **by appointment,** as soon as possible after initial contact. It involves commitment and when you obligate yourself, keep the appointment.

F. Witnessing teams should meet every evening at 6:00 p.m. to go out and contact the names given during the revival.

II. **Promotion and Publicity** - This will attract some of the faithful but will not usually attract the lost people. It is needed to enhance, but not as a foundation. **It will take personal contact to draw people.**

A. Use the church sign or marquis

B. Use a newspaper ad with a story.

C. Use radio spots, announcements or the television

D. Use leaflets or fliers

E. Use the telephone, use well-known ladies or men in the church. Call all members.

All publicity must exalt the person of Jesus Christ.

III. **Spiritual Preparation**

A. Encourage people to pray for the revival and the lost persons they know. There is no substitute for being specific with God.

B. Cottage prayer meetings may be arranged as designated by leadership.

C. Encourage family prayer meetings for the revival.

D. Daily constantly pray together - using the telephone also to pray for the success of the revival.

E. Fast and pray for the revival.

F. Designate certain passages or scriptures from the Bible by the pastor to read on a daily basis leading up to the revival.

G. Start sharing Christ and sowing the seed of invitation a week or several weeks prior to the revival.

Witnessing Procedure and Follow-up Approach

By the Street Ministry, Inc.

"It Happens After Prayer." You should always pray first for forgiveness of sins, then to be filled and led of the Holy Spirit asking God to save souls or people and to make you fruitful, before you attempt to witness.

Then you should pair off into two(s) or three(s), choosing before hand who will do the witnessing and who will be the silent partner. The silent partner is the individual who prays, keeps order, and keeps silent unless asked to speak by the person doing the witnessing.

After you approach the prospect, you should introduce yourself.

Example: I am __________, a member of the_________ Church and this is _______________(partner) and we are taking a religious survey. We would like to take a few minutes of your time and share some scriptures with you and ask several questions.

Prospect: I don't have much time.

Worker: May we have at least five minutes?

If the answer is still no, ask the prospect this question:

If you were to die in the next five minutes, where would you spend eternity, heaven or hell?

If the response is still negative, leave a biblical tract with the prospect and try to set up another appointment if the Lord so leads you to do so.

Prospect: *Yes, come in.*

Worker: **Thank you.**

Once you are in the house, establish rappört with the prospect. Talk about the weather, baby, furniture, house, etc. After rapport has been established ask this question:

Example: _____, concerning spiritual matters, allow me to ask you this question: "If you were to die in the next five minutes, where would you spend eternity, heaven or hell?"

Note: Any response other than a positive "Yes, I would go to Heaven," the person witnessing should go directly to **St. John 3:16**, after receiving the prospects permission. Be sure to explain to them that the Bible is the perfect word of God and it is essential they believe the Bible, the Holy Scriptures.

Worker: The first thing (Mr. or Mrs.____________) that God would have you to know is that He loves you.

> **"For God so loved the world, that he gave his only begotten Son, that whosoever believeth in him should not perish, but have everlasting life." St. John 3:16**

Worker: **You do agree, that "God Loves You", don't you?**

Prospect: *Yes.*

Worker: It is also true that you are a sinner and you were born in sin.

> **"For all have sinned, and come short of the glory of God;" Romans 3:23**

All that is not righteous is sin. In the sight of God, you are a lost sinner because you were born in sin according to Psalms 51:5.

Worker: Do you agree with the Word of God that you are a sinner?

Prospect: *Yes.*

Worker: It is also true that you are dead in sin spiritually, not physically, because your sins have separated you from God.

> **"For the wages of sin is death;" Romans 6:23a**

You are dead in sin until you accept Christ as your personal Savior. If you remain in sin, then you will spend eternity in hell, which is the second death or eternal death. Romans 6:23a

Now you know that God loves you, and that you are a sinner dead in sin. Before we go to the next point, do you agree with what we have covered so far?

Prospect: *Yes.*

Worker: Thank God for this truth found in:

> **Romans 5:6, "For when we were yet without strength, in due time Christ died for the ungodly".**

Christ died for you. Christ bore your sins in is own body on the cross. Do you believe Christ died at Calvary for you?

Prospect: Yes

Worker: According to I Cor.15:1-4 , He was buried and rose again according to the scriptures. Not only did God bring Him back to life again, but He ascended and is at the right hand of God, as Lord.

Worker: Since you know that Christ died for you, you may be asking yourself, "What must I do to be saved from hell and delivered from my sins"?

> **Acts 16:31 tells us, "And they said, Believe on the Lord Jesus Christ, and thou shalt be saved, and thy house".**

This scripture proves you can be saved or delivered of wrong doing by exercising faith or trust on the Lord Jesus Christ, and that is, taking Him at His word. Heart belief, not intellectual belief, counts. James 2:19

See, (Mr. or Mrs. __________________), when you confess with your mouth that Jesus is Lord and believe from your heart that God hath raised him from the dead, according to Romans 10:9, you will be saved.

Worker: Do you believe from your heart that Jesus is the Christ, the Savior, the Son of the Living God who came in flesh? I John. 4:2

Prospect: Yes.

(If the answer is "no" leave a tract and pray for the prospect if you are allowed, and find someone else).

Worker: Accept Him now by faith and pray this prayer: Lord Jesus, I am a sinner, forgive me of all my sins, come into my heart and save me. I do now confess you as my Risen Lord. Thank you Lord for saving me. Rom. 10:13

Ask them if this prayer expresses the desire of their heart? If so, lead them into this prayer letting them know that by just repeating words will not save them but having faith in Christ will bring salvation, forgiveness, and joy and a brand new beginning.

Worker: Mr. or Mrs.____________________, did you sincerely ask Christ Jesus to come into your heart?

Prospect: Yes.

Worker: Did you mean it?

Prospect: Yes!

Worker: What did Christ do?

Prospect: He came into my heart. He saved me. He delivered me. He forgave me.

Worker: Then according to Acts 5:29b, "We ought to obey God rather than men".

Worker: My friend, determine now to obey your Lord and Master Jesus Christ in all things.

1. You need to, as soon as possible unite with a Bible believing church - Acts 2:47. (Invite the convert to your church).

2. You need to follow Him in the Ordinance of Baptism - Acts 2:41.

3. You need to join a Sunday School Class to study God's Word - II Timothy 2:15.

4. You need to attend worship service to enjoy the fellowship with other saints - Hebrews 10:25.

5. You need to give, as the Lord prospers you according to I Corinthians 16:1,2.

6. You need to pray by the Spirit and continue in prayer daily - I Thessalonians 5:17.

7. You need to tell others that the Lord Jesus Christ has saved and delivered you - St. John 4:39.

8. You need to read God's Word to grow in grace and in knowledge that you may be a faithful Christian - II Peter 3:18.

9. Start reading I John, a chapter a day, then the book of St. John or another book of the Bible. Guidance is the important factor in the life of a new convert.

Follow-up Procedures

by Street Ministry, Inc.

1. Invite them to attend church with you.
2. Let them know that you will pick them up at an agreed time.
3. Mr. or Mrs. ____________________ according to Hebrews 10:25,

   "Not forsaking the assembling of ourselves together, as the manner of some is; but exhorting one another: and so much the more, as ye see the day approaching".

   This is a commandment from God and you will obey it if Jesus is in your heart.
4. Encourage them to enroll in a Sunday School Class, or set up a Bible study in their home as quickly as possible. The first twenty-four hours are the most crucial in the life of a new convert. If Bible studies have been established in the home, then start with:

   (A) The Plan of Salvation (Assurance)

   (B) How to study the Bible

   (C) How to pray

   (D) Church Membership

   (E) How to walk in the Spirit

(F) How to Witness and give their testimony

(G) How to overcome temptation, by running from sin, praying, focusing the mind on other things, and by resisting Satan by quoting the Word of God

Teach the convert how to receive cleansing from their sins, how to understand trials and persecutions, and how to know God's Will for their life.

5. Before leaving the new converts, join hands in prayer and leave a good biblical tract for them to read with your name,church name, and phone number.

6. At this point, be sure to fill out the information card completely.

7. Regardless of when witnessing is done, be sure to go by and see them the next day. Remind them that they should make a public decision in identifying with the church. Reassure them that this is what the Lord would have them to do according to His Word. Most of all encourage them and explain to them the ways of "temptation and trouble".

8. Pick them up and sit with them through worship service, if possible. If not, get someone spiritual to sit with them through the service.

9. During the invitation invite them to make a public decision. Tell them if they are afraid to walk to the pulpit area, or front alone, you will go to the front with them. But please, do not force them to make a premature decision.

10. They should be picked up and worked with by the worker until they are strong enough to make it on their own. Two-three months of studying from the Master Outlines in the Christian Life New Testament will be very helpful. By this time if they are real, a decision to become a part of a local church should be accomplished.

Helpful Points In Witnessing

1. Don't get off the subject. Point to Christ and emphasize the Resurrection.
2. Watch the time. Do not get bogged down.
3. Don't witness or teach too fast. A baby feeds from a bottle not a fire hose.
4. Do not give him too much material at one time. It takes a lifetime to produce a Christian.
5. Avoid controversial questions. Stay with the fundamentals of faith.
6. Don't go unprepared, II Timothy 2:15. If you don't know, say that. The answer to the question can be given later.
7. Watch bad breath. Teeth care is very important if you are going to communicate the gospel.
8. Do not bring gloom into the convert's home, Galatians 5:22. The joy of God is catching.
9 Don't witness or teach with a "know-it-all" attitude. It is all right not to know everything about God and the Bible. Continue to learn and grow in God's

grace, love, mercy, revelation, understanding and knowledge.

10. Don't argue, II Timothy 2:16.

PLAN OF SALVATION

By Dr. Jayel Jacobs, Jr.

Approach: My name is__________, we're taking a Christian Survey, may we have a few minutes of your time?

Get on common ground, example: weather, home, children, etc.

May I have permission to give my personal testimony?

Give your personal testimony as to how you got saved.

Have you heard?

I. God is Love, John 3:16.

Remember to read the scriptures and give interpretation. (The world means mankind. Perish means hell.)

II. God loves sinning people, Romans 3:23. (I have sinned and you have sinned.)

III. If you remain in sin, you will go to hell, Romans 6:23. (Wages means penalty.)

IV. Your part in being saved is to...

   A. Repent and acknowledge you are wrong, Luke 13:5. (Turn to God) .

B. Believe and trust in what God says, Acts 16:30-31, I Cor. 15:1-4. (Share the gospel.)

He ascended, Acts 1:9.

He's seated, Col. 3:1.

He is Lord, I Cor. 12:3 (Supreme Authority.)

Repeat - Do you believe Jesus Christ died for your sins so that you may have the forgiveness of your sins?

Now your aim or goal is: ***To get them to invite Christ in their heart, or life - Rev. 3:20***

Say something like this:

There is a knob on the inside of your heart, you should invite the Lord to come in, to forgive you of your sins, and be willing to turn from your sins to God.

Ask if they are ready to invite Christ in their lives. Have them to pray for forgiveness, for Christ to come in, and declare to Him they are willing to turn from sins.

V. Confession is a Result of Being Saved.

I John 4:2-3

Romans 10:9

I Corinthians 12:3

Test them: *Ask them what did they do?*

How do they know they are saved?

Who saved them?

Have them to make their confession.

Confession: Jesus Christ is the Son of God who came in the flesh. Jesus Christ died on the cross for my sins, was buried, and rose again. He ascended back to God, as Lord.

VI. **Water Baptism - Mark 16:16**

They need to be told to follow the Lord Jesus Christ in baptism immediately.

VII. **Unite with a Bible Believing Church. - Heb. 10:25**

Make sure you get their name, address, telephone number, and landmark or location.

Invitation Procedures

- *Take the initiative as directed by the Pastor.*
- *Check inquirers as they come down. Ask them, "What did you have in mind when you came down?"*
- *Repentance - need for forgiveness I John 1:9*
- *Prayer - Matthew 7:7ff*
- *Guidelines for when people come down:*

1. *Help them Walk in the Spirit. Romans 8:1-4*
2. *Show them God's two basic wills are for us to walk in Him I Thessalonians 4:3-7 and witness of Him - Acts 1:8*
3. *To surrender, separate, and create in him/her a desire to do His will. Philippians 2:13*
4. *And If they want the opportunity for:*

   salvation, restoration to fellowship, assurance, membership with the church, and transfer of membership, deal with them in the counseling room or as directed by the Pastor. Philippians 2:3-5

Follow-up Procedures

On New and Inactive Members

by the worker

Paul showed us how to intercede. He said, "**And this I pray, that your love may abound yet more and more in knowledge and in all judgment;" Philippians 1:9**

Example: "Lord, make me a channel of love. Give me wisdom, and engineer circumstances in their lives to draw them to you, and reveal to me their needs."

Objective:
Follow-up is used to see to it that the lost are not only converted, but also that they are going on with Christ in the life of the church family.

1. Follow-up must be done within 24 hours of the decision.

2. The follow-up person must:

 Demonstrate a genuine interest in the person.

 Be a good listener with an understanding heart. (Never argue)

Get to know and love the person.

Pray daily for the person. When you can, pray with them.

3. Go over study materials and give assurance and instruction concerning their decision.

4. Encourage them to be faithful in Sunday Morning Bible Study, Morning Worship, and Prayer Meeting.

5. Urge them to:

•**Pray daily.** (Have a prayer time) Matthew 26:41

•**Read and study the Bible daily.** Acts 17:11 Psalms 119:11

•**Stress the importance of fellowship with other believers.** - Hebrews 10:25

•**Stress God's will for everyone is to walk in Him and witness of Him, as they grow**.

I Thessalonians 4:2-7; Acts 1:8

•**Help them to seek the attributes of Jesus Christ.**

Luke 22:42; Philippians 2:5-13

6. Keep a check on them and their faithfulness.

7. Help them to start attending church regularly, studying, praying, witnessing with their lives, and doing evangelism.

8. Help them to help others to attend church, study the Bible, pray, and witness to friends, relatives, and other lost relationships.

Standard Program for Crusades

Devotion - 15 minutes

Master of Ceremony in Charge

Congregational Song (Led by Master of Ceremony)

Choir selection - 5 to 15 minutes

Testimony or Testimonies - 5 minutes

Offering (Play Soft Music)

Solo

Scripture

Prayer

Choir

Sermon

Invitation

Benediction

Special Important Notes

The general principle of this program is to allow the Evangelist to preach as soon as possible.

Testimonies: Testimonies should not be longer than 5 minutes. These people will be selected in advance. Testimonies should be of what the Lord has done for you - not a sermon. These people will sit on the platform with the ministers (although this is optional).

Offering: **The Master of Ceremony should stress to the people to give liberally.**

Invitation: **The Evangelist preaching will give the invitation.**

The people who come will be prayed for in one general prayer. Afterwards they will be sent to the counseling area.

Christian Life Missionary Baptist Church, a Light in the dark.

Summary

Rev. Willie Barnes, a Pastor in Galveston, Texas made this statement to me as we were talking about the preparation of this book. He stated, "Your life has been Evangelism." In this book, portions of my life's story were told with an emphasis on evangelism, as an Evangelist and as a Pastor.

Evangelism begins with God, because He creates and calls us into His Ministry. God prepares us for our contribution in society and the Church. We should never warehouse what we have learned, especially that which concerns evangelism.

I have discovered that evangelism is something that must be done in the power of the Holy Spirit. It has been stated, that every believer has the responsibility to evangelize. The pastor has the responsibility not only, to disciple others in Christ, but also to do the work of an evangelist. There are many lessons learned on the way as a person prepares to do the work of the church, which is to evangelize. Praying, studying, giving, witnessing, and giving in faith are essentials for successful evangelism.

"*From Preaching on the Streets to Pastoring in the Pulpit,*" suggests some methods that might be helpful in evangelism. Remember that evangelism and follow-up are running partners.

Evangelism will never be a reality without the new race loving God, and being willing to do what the Lord has commanded in His Great Commission.

> **Matthew 28:19-20, "Go ye therefore, and teach all nations, baptizing them in the name of the Father, and of the Son, and of the Holy Ghost:**
>
> **Teaching them to observe all things whatsoever I have commanded you: and, lo, I am with you alway, even unto the end of the world. Amen."**

Christian Life, a church that believes in practicing the principles of biblical economics which produces great results.

TESTIMONIES

The effectiveness of evangelism can best be shown through the following testimonies:

Evangelism Through a Bible Study

The most memorable experience for me was in the Street Ministry days, when my witnessing partner and I were teaching a Bible class, in an apartment complex. As we began to present the plan of salvation to one of the sisters, her other two sisters entered the house, and all three were led to the Lord Jesus Christ. We referred the young ladies to a local church and they became members. One of the young ladies told us later, that her boyfriend was in the back room and he believed the gospel and was saved too.

The Unusual at a Funeral

As I reminisce all the blessings and miracles I have seen for fourteen years at Christian Life, I am reminded that Pastor Jacobs is definitely a true man of God. He is one who believes in prayer. During one Wednesday night prayer meeting, the Holy Spirit's power fell upon the congregation. People all over the sanctuary were crying and praising the Lord. As the Spirit began to move we said one by one, "All that I have belongs to God, and He can have it all." I recall the Pastor turning in the direction of the organ asking the question, "Does this mean your husband too?" I replied, "yes". Three weeks later, my husband was killed. From that day on, I listened closely to every word of God that came out of a true man of God's mouth. It is awesome to see God use a man who is so evangelistic at heart and in mind, such as, Dr. Jacobs. His constant aim is to see people saved from hell, sin, and Satan. I asked the Pastor to preach the eulogy at the funeral. After the eulogy, he gave an invitation and I saw many people saved. Families were re-united, many asked for forgiveness, and others came back to the church. I saw one of the most unorthodox things that I have ever seen at a funeral. Pastor Jacobs said, God told him to take up an offering. At the close of the funeral service, the Lord had given me, through His people, thousands of dollars. Pastor Jacobs has always believed that it happens after prayer. This statement is true because God has and is mending my wounds, healing my body, and giving me peace.

Evangelism in the Front Door of a Church

While we were on a tour in Mississippi, we stopped after driving most of the day. The Pastor suggested that we drive around the city looking for people to share Christ. We went down the street to a neighborhood that was located right behind a church. We had the opportunity to witness to several elderly people. While I was witnessing to a lady about 80 years old, on her front porch, it seemed like the Devil pulled me off the porch trying to injure me, before I led her to the Lord. The lady prayed to receive Christ that night. We encouraged her to go to the church closest to her home. The Pastor made the observation that the church needs to look out of its door and see its neighbors. That is when I truly realized that people needed to be witnessed to, even in the front door of a church building.

The Power of Unified Evangelism

We witness every Saturday afternoon as a church. One Saturday, we went to several different areas. As we traveled and stopped, there were more than 100 people from our church walking, singing, praying, and passing out tracts in each complex as we went witnessing. Just before a rain storm came that evening, the Lord used the Pastor to preach and pray for the people. As a result, we saw many saved.

Evangelism Can Be Done Anywhere

On New Years Eve 1996, the Pastor led us to the streets to preach and do spiritual warfare. While preaching in the direction of a club, a lady drove up on her way to a New Year's Eve party. She told us that she had heard us and decided to come over to where we were. Some of the women in the church witnessed to her and that night she received Christ into her life. Praise God!

It Happens after Prayer

One Sunday morning, during an invitation in 1985, a young man, approximately thirteen years old collapsed as we stood around the pulpit. He appeared not to be breathing, and there seemed to be no sign of life. Some of the people in the congregation called for a doctor or a nurse. Pastor Jacobs pressed his way through the congregation and said, "You better call on God." At that time he prayed, and immediately the boy opened his eyes, and began to breath. Glory be to God, he was able to continue the worship service!

Evangelism Will Happen If You Go

In 1989, a group from our church went to Little Rock, Arkansas with Dr. Jacobs to witness and share Christ. We went to an apartment complex where the Pastor preached and witnessed to the people there. The apartment complex was infested with drugs, alcohol, and immorality. Many of those who heard the message came to know Jesus Christ as their Lord. Seven years later, we returned to Little Rock and discovered that the same apartment complex had been closed down. God had once again answered our prayers. He shut down the Devil's territory.

Evangelism Brings about a Change

For many years, Dr. Jacobs had led the Street Ministry and the Christian Life Missionary Baptist Church to the streets of northeast Oklahoma City and other areas. I have observed God transforming the northeast side of Oklahoma City, into something wonderful. The same streets we preached, witnessed, and did spiritual warfare on have been renovated and new businesses established. I believe God is honoring Dr. Jacobs and his work in that area.

Nothing is too Hard for God

One Sunday night while having service in the Willie Wilson building, a young lady came running down to the sanctuary with her son in her arms, and handed him to the Pastor. The Pastor took the baby and lifted him up to the Lord. God heard his prayer and revived the baby. We began to praise God. Pastor Jacobs said that he was glad that she did not run out the door, but ran to God.

Evangelism for All

While in the Street Ministry, we took a trip to Nashville, Tennessee. We arrived there and could not find a room anywhere, so we went to a restaurant. While there, the Pastor and a group of our men were approached by some homosexuals. We observed, but did not witness to them. On our way to the next city, the Pastor had us to stop and get out of the van, on the side of a country road, and pray for forgiveness. The Pastor said, "We would never make that mistake again," and that we would witness to all people.

Fruitful Evangelism from Door-to-Door

Seventeen years ago, Pastor Jacobs and members of the Street Ministry showed up at my house. My life was changed forever. I am so very grateful that Dr. Jacobs followed the Lord's direction in evangelizing. I had visited a church a few weeks earlier and left vowing in my heart and mind, that I would never step foot into a church again. God sent someone, because He knew that I needed salvation. Thank God I received Christ that day!

Sent to Millions to Get One

We witnessed in Houston, Texas for hours and no one had accepted Christ. At our last location, one young man received Christ. I remember the Pastor saying, "God sent us all the way to Houston, Texas for one soul." Two weeks later, the mother of the young man sent a praise report on her son's new life.

Deliverance, God's Specialty

After twelve years of being at Christian Life, my Pastor has done wonderful things to make a positive effect on my life. My oldest son was born and diagnosed as having spinal meningitis. His fever was over 104 degrees. I remember Pastor praying and asking God to deliver him from this attack of Satan. The next morning, my wife, and I went back to the hospital and our son was up playing with his "I.V." tubing and smiling. The doctors did not find any more signs of the illness. We thanked and praised God for what He had done, and we thanked God for having a Pastor with the courage to pray.

Love, Something Done

After the April 19, 1995 bombing of the Oklahoma City Alfred P. Murrah building, our Pastor led us to sing, embrace, and love those who were hurting at the bombing site for twelve days. One woman stood out above the rest as I hugged her she replied, "I have never hugged an African American before this time. My parents were prejudiced and so was I until now," she cried aloud. As my arms embraced her I could feel the pain from her heart. The white lady approximately 35 years old, thanked our Pastor and our Church for being there to love in a special way.

Evangelism Calms A City

In the summer of 1985, our Pastor, being led by the Holy Spirit led us to N.E. 23rd and Martin Luther King every Sunday evening, to encourage and love the youth of Oklahoma City. At that time, it was a hang out strip for thousands of youth. Many denied their gang affiliation, put away their guns, and came to Christ. During that time, youth were killing one another on N.E. 23rd Street. After much prayer and preaching, the power of God caused the killings to stop in that area.

God Meets Needs Through Others

Over the years, Pastor Jacobs has given my family thousands of dollars. Each time he was moved by God to give to us, it was definitely needed. The first time God used him to give to me will always be special. I was trying to get back in the Army Reserve in 1986. We were expecting a child, and my family needed the money for numerous bills. The solution God had given me was to return to the Army Reserves. However, being an officer, I had to buy all of my uniforms and equipment. I remember walking down the hallway of the church, and talking to the Pastor about my problems. Before I could finish talking, he reached into his pocket and gave me the exact amount of money I needed. I had never experienced someone who was not family giving to me without asking. Over the years Dr. Jacobs has done many wonderful things for me, but this occurrence will always be remembered by me.

Evangelism Reaching Far and Near

The Lord allowed the bus ministry to evangelize at the Guthrie Job Corp. Center in Guthrie, Oklahoma. We witnessed on campus and picked up students consistently for approximately three years. The buses were filled to capacity. I recall on several occasions, having 88 students on Sunday morning. These students came from all over the southern part of the United States. Hundreds were saved doing this three year period of time, and they also became active in the church.

Evangelism through a Bus Ministry

The days with the Street Ministry had so many happy events. I remember God used me to lead 21 souls to Christ during a revival. My greatest memory, I think, would be driving a 72 passenger bus, loaded with kids taking them to the study house every Monday. Who would have thought that 20 years later, there would be young men and women coming up to me saying, "You don't remember me do you?" They would say, "Remember you use to pick me up on that big yellow bus and take me to the study house." One of the men, I saw recently, told me that he was preaching the gospel. Another young lady I met was a nurse and several others were in college or married and raising their families in the Oklahoma City area. Who would have thought, that driving a big yellow bus would have made such a difference in so many young lives.

Evangelism in a Revival

The most memorable occasion of the Street Ministry was a revival at New Hope Baptist Church in Langston, Oklahoma. I was in my first semester at Langston University. There were people witnessing on the campus all that week. They asked me, "If you were to die in the next five minutes, where would you spend eternity, heaven or hell?" This was my first time away from home without anyone watching me, and where I would spend eternity was not on my mind at that time. Every night my cousins would go to the revival, and I would go to a party. They always came back excited about the revival. Finally, I decided to go. At the revival, the students were testifying as to what God had done for them that week. A young lady during the service sung, " I Must Tell Jesus." That night, it seemed as though God was only speaking to me. After the sermon by Evangelist Jacobs, entitled, "One More Night with the Frogs", I accepted Christ.

Christian Life Missionary Baptist Church sanctuary ceiling view of the lighted cross representing the good news of Jesus Christ's resurrection.

Evangelist Jayel Jacobs Jr. following the mandate of the Lord Jesus Christ.

Praise The Lord !

Special Recognition

People will not forget you, if you meet their needs in a storm. God uses people to meet the needs of His people. The Lord taught me to trust Him for my needs. I had to literally depend on the Lord day by day. God used churches and organizations to send donations to continue His work. Southwest Independent Baptist Church and Dr. Bert Harrison, the Pastor, played a tremendous part in my ministry. This southside church supported us monthly, taught us about the work of a bus ministry, through Bro. Ludie Smith, and introduced us to supporting missionary work around the world.

Other financial support for the Street Ministry came from my brother, Walter C. Jacobs, stationed in Anchorage, Alaska in the Air Force. He had a $28.75 allotment sent every month for years in support of my family and the Lord's work.

St. James Baptist Church, where I was a member, under the leadership of Pastor W.B. Parker, during my Street Ministry tenure, was the first to commit to $150.00 each month until the Holy Spirit brought Christian Life into existence.

Progressive Baptist State Convention, Inc., and President Dr. T.J. Roberts supported our ministry along with the Concerned Clergy for Spiritual Renewal under the leadership of Dr. M.A. Curry. The Baptist Ministerial

Association and President Rev. J.B. Bratton also supported our ministry monthly along with the Emmanuel Baptist Church. Later, the B.M.A. continued their support under the leadership of President T.H. Hubbard.

Many churches and some organizations stood with us as we followed the Lord, such as, New Hope of Langston, OK, Pastor J.D. Ford; Greater Marshall Memorial Baptist Church, Pastor Moses Howard, Jr.; Unity Baptist Church, Pastor Eric Mayes; St. Luke Baptist Church, Pastor Dewitt Roland; Shiloh Baptist Church, Pastor T.H. Hubbard; Mt. Olive Baptist Church, Pastor E.R. Neal; and Providence Nazarene, Pastor Joe Edwards.

I cannot fail to mention others who allowed me to preach in revival meetings such as the Wildewood Christian Church, Pastor Simms; McKinley Avenue Independent Baptist Church, Pastor Lonnie Gee; Fairview Baptist Church, Pastor J.A. Reed; Timothy Baptist, Tulsa, OK, Pastor J.C. Gilkey; Mt. Zion Baptist Church, Pastor Dr. G.C. McCutchen; Faith Memorial Baptist Church, Pastor M.A. Curry; Emmanuel Baptist Church, Chicago, IL., Pastor L.A. Curry; New Hope Baptist Church, Pastor J.D. Provo; New Hope Baptist Church, Pastor Allen Johnson, Galveston, TX; and friend, Rev. Willie Barnes, now Pastor of the Mt. Gilead Baptist Church in Galveston, TX.

Others Supporters included: Pastor Willie Bates of Central Baptist Church, in Chandler, OK and Oklahoma City; Pastor Willie Boone, Jr. and Pleasant Ridge Baptist Church; Pastor Dr. C.C. Carroll of the Mt. Moriah Baptist Church; Pastor Dr. W.K. Jackson and St. John Missionary

Baptist Church, who supported us in many ways throughout my ministry; Union Baptist Church, Shawnee, OK and Pastor Dr. Cliet Wilburn; Pastor Leroy Davis and Morning Star Baptist Church, Anadarko, OK; Pastor W.F. Denton, Mt. Elam Baptist Church; Pastor Lovis Mays, First Baptist Church, Luther, OK; Rev. Louis Parker, Assistant Pastor at St. James Baptist Church; Rev. Sampson Moore, Harrison Baptist Church; Rev. J.S. Ross, Siloam Missionary Baptist Church; St. Matthew Baptist Church, Eagletown, OK; Rev. W.K. Arnold and Paradise Baptist Church; Rev. Eddie Baker and Tabitha Baptist Church; and Rev. O.B. Burrough and Hillwood Baptist Church.

I also owe a great debt of gratitude to Rev. Stacy Cowan in Dallas, Texas; Sis. Verlene Farmer of the Baptist Student Union of Langston University; Sis. W.O. Merrell, a member of Southwest Baptist Church; Rev. Bob Lovejoy of the Home Mission Board for the Southern Baptist Convention of Oklahoma City; and the Capital Baptist Association under the leadership of Rev. Ernest Perkins.

I could not have made it without the faithful support and care of members of The Street Ministry Inc. They were: Joyce Jacobs, Shirley Nero, Irene Jenkins, Bobby Joe Jacobs, Linda Jacobs, Renae Parker, Claudia Gillespie, Leroy Gillespie, Lillian Stoner, Estella Nero, Marshaline Ford, Charla Goss, Doug Pendarvis, Gail Wilburn, Cliet Wilburn, Kevin Hobbs, Pat Hobbs, Sandra Bowser, Elmer Bowser, Shirley Williams, Marsha Lou Jackson, Wanzetta Woody, Faye Macon, Walter Jacobs, the Ford Family, Jimmie McEwen, Sandra Miller, Irene Wilson, Sherry Taylor, Sandra Harris, Raymond Wandick, Laura Hopgood,

Daniel Humphrey, Glenda Ford, Karen Moore, Valorie Coleman, Johnny Moore, Clorette Woody, Virgie Johnson, Debra Coulter, Clotiel Ford, Linda Smith, Lawrence and Beverly Kirk, Claude Woody, Florence Harris, Jackie Humphrey, Frankie Humphrey, Brenda Horton, Barbara Shannon and others.

Members of the Christian Life Missionary Baptist Church Youth Ministry

This is a scene from the drama, "For We May Never Know." Over 200 young people received the Lord and were baptized throughout Oklahoma and Kansas.

SERMON TOPICS

by Dr. Jayel Jacobs, Jr.

1. Subject: "This Is It, Do You Want It?"
   Text: John 5:24

2. Subject: "Do What You Can"
   Text: Mark 6:1-6

3. Subject: "An Acceptable Offering"
   Text: II Corinthians 8: 1 ff

4. Subject: "The Blessed Hope"
   Text: I Corinthians 15:19ff

5. Subject: "Moving The Hand Of God Through Giving"
   Text: I Samuel 1:7-19

6. Subject: "Prevention From The Biblical Perspective"
   Text: Luke 1:28ff

7. Subject: "What A True Pastor Wants You To Know"
   Text: Hebrews 13:17

8. Subject: "Use What You Have"
   Text: Luke 9:10-17

9. Subject: "Toiling, But Catching Nothing"
   Text: Luke 5: 1 -11

10. Subject: "Saved By Grace"
    Text: Ephesians 2:8-11

11. Subject: "Why?"
    Text: Matthew 27:46b

12. Subject: "The Role Of The Holy Spirit In Soul-winning"
    Text: Acts 1:8

13. Subject: "The Productivity Of Humility"
    Text: I Peter 5:5-6

14. Subject: "How The Man Of Color Survived"
    Text: Romans 8:32-39

15. Subject: "A True Disciple"
    Text: Matthew 16:24-28

16. Subject: "Face It With God"
    Text: Proverbs 3:5; Psalms 147:3

17. Subject: "Give God The Glory"
    Text: Romans 11:28-36

18. Subject: "Love, The Missing Ingredient"
    Text: I Corinthians 13:4-8

19. Subject: "Satisfied With Jesus Christ"
    Text: Philippians 2:5-11

20. Subject: "If God Be For You!"
    Text: Romans 8:3 1 b

21. Subject: "Remember Who's In The Boat With You"
    Text: Mark 4:35-40

22. Subject: "Be A Copy Cat"
    Text: Ephesians 5:14-18

23. Subject: "Why, You Need The Church"
    Text: Hebrews 11:25

24. Subject: "The Command"
    Text: Matthew 28:18-20

25. Subject: "A Truly Good Husband"
    Text: Ephesians 5:2-5

26. Subject: "A New Race"
    Text: Ephesians 2:11-17

27. Subject: "Shifting From Your Condition To Your Position"
    Text: Ephesians 2:5,6-1 Colossians 1:21-22; 3:2-3

28. Subject: "One More Night With The Frogs"
    Text: Exodus 8:6-106

29. Subject: "Beware of Voices on Broadway"
    Text: Proverbs 7:1-21

30. Subject: "Unconditional Love"
    Text: I Corinthians 13

31. Subject: "Don't Let It Happen To You.
    Text: Matthew 7:21-23
    (My first sermon)

A Youth Retreat is an excellent opportunity to evangelize and win young people to Christ. Two accepted Jesus Christ on this occasion.

Christian Life Missionary Baptist Church young people singing to the glory of God.

Quotations

1. "It Happens After Prayer"
2. "I Can't Hear What You Say, For Seeing What You Do"
3. "That's What Your Mouth Says"
4. "Tough Times Don't Last, But Tough People Do"
5. "It Happens After Praise"
6. "It Happens After Thanksgiving"
7. "Don't Go There"
8. "Get The Bird In Hand"
9. "Is This Getting In Your Spirit"
10. "Come In Here"
11. "There Is No Substitute For Giving"
12. "You Can't Grow An Oak Tree Over Night"
13. "Busy Doing Chores, Rather Than, The Work Of The Church"
14. "If Not The Church, Who?"

15. "Hang Tuff"
16. "Love Won't Fail To Evangelize"
17. "Jesus, Lord Jesus, Jesus Got It Going On"
18. "Haul Off And Do It"
19. "Don't You See"
20. "Don't Quit"
21. "Cut The Cake"
22. "Do It God's Way"
23. "I'm Depending On You"
24. "I'm Godly Proud Of You"
25. "I'm Not Going Back To Egypt"
26. "The Darkest Hour Is Just Before Day"
27. "The Best Is Yet To Come"
28. "It's Going To Be All Right"
29. "Hello!"
30. "Watch Your Friend And Your Kin"
31. "Pray About Everything, Worry About Nothing"
32. "Now, Isn't That Wonderful"

33. "Murmuring Is Negative Confession"

34. "Change Begins In The Leader First"

35. "Healthy Growth Takes Time, The Spirit's Time"

36. "But God"

37. "In The Morning"

38. "Help Is On The Way"

39. "Don't Get Weary"

40. "You Don't Hear Me"

41. "Stay Together"

42. "One Leader At A Time"

43. "A Quitter Never Wins And A Winner Never Quits"

44. "Somebody Took That"

45. "Time Will Tell"

46. "It's To Early To Tell'

47. "In The Morning"

48. "Get Home Before Dark"

49. "There Is Power In Unity"

50. "Love, The Key That Unlocks The Door"

Unity line formed on NE 23rd & Martin Luther King Street to the Capitol against Crime.

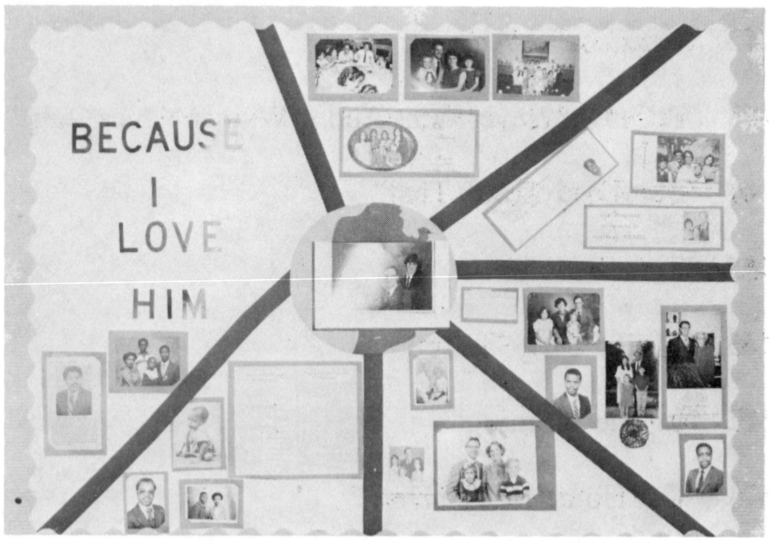

Missionaries and Extensions that Christian Life Missionary Baptist Church supported financially.

Special Thanks

Rev. C.C. Abram - Mt. Lebanon Baptist Church
Rev. M. Abrams - Solid Rock C.O.G.I.C.
Rev. J. Anderson - Pleasant Ridge Baptist Church
Rev. W. K. Arnold - Paradise Baptist Church
Rev. I.L. Bacy - New Bethel Baptist Church
Rev. E. Baker - Tabitha Baptist Church
Rev. W. Barnes & Family - Mt. Gilead Baptist, Galveston, TX
Rev. W. Bates - Central Baptist Church
Rev. J. Berry - Tabernacle Baptist Church
Rev. A. A. Bolten - First Baptist Church, Green Pastures
Rev. E. E. Booker - Mt. Olive Baptist Church
Rev. C. Boone - St. James Baptist Church
Rev. W. Boone, Jr. - Pleasant Ridge Baptist Church
Rev. J. O. Bradford - Fifth Street Baptist Church
Dr. J. B. Bratton - Emmanuel Baptist Church
Rev. C. Broadous - Sixth Street Christian Church
Dr. B. Bright - Campus Crusade for Christ, Sacramento, CA
Rev. R.C. Brown - Christian Faith Fellowship
Rev. O. B. Burrough - Hillwood Baptist Church
Rev. D. Burton - St. Paul Baptist Church, Green Pastures
Dr. T. D. Callendar - Johnson Memorial Bible Institute
Rev. C.T. Carrington - A.M.E Methodist Church, Arcadia Oklahoma
Dr. C. C. Carroll - Emmanuel Baptist Church
Rev. C. Carruthers - Christian Life Missionary Baptist Church
Rev. J. Carruthers - ElReno Prison Ministry
Rev.. J. Coats - Bethlehem Star Baptist Church
Dr. T.O. Chappelle - Oklahoma State Baptist Convention
Dr. C. Clark - Baptist Temple Church, Tulsa, OK

Special Thanks

Dr. M. Colby - Victory Temple C.O.G.I.C.

Dr. J. Coleman - Langston University, Professor

Dr. D. Cottner - Central America University Ministries, Inc., Kansas City, KS

Rev. S. Cowan - Street Ministry Inc., Dallas, TX

Rev. G. Cunningham - Metropolitan Church

Dr. L. C. Curry - Emmanuel Baptist Church, Chicago, IL

Dr. M. A. Curry - Faith Memorial Baptist Church

Rev. W. Dallas - Mt. Zion Baptist Church, Stillwater, OK

Dr. C. Davis - Tabernacle Baptist Church

Rev. L. Davis - Morning Star Baptist Church, Anadarko, OK

Dr. J. H. Davis - Calvary Baptist Church

Rev. S. Davidson - Southwest Baptist Church

Rev.. C. B. Dawson - Little Rock Baptist Church, Inc., Brooklyn, NY

Rev. W. Dean - Mt. Zion Baptist Church, Stillwater, OK

Rev. W. L. Denton - Mt. Elam Baptist Church

Rev. L. Doaks - Mt. Pilgrim Baptist Church

Rev. C. Douglas - Living Word Missionary Baptist Church

Dr. J. Edwards - Providence Nazarene Church

Rev. F. Elkins - Fifth Street Baptist Church

Rev. K. Ellis - Galilee Baptist Church

Rev. Z. R. Finley - Mt. Lebanon Baptist Church

Dr. R. Fish - Professor of Evangelism, Southwestern Theological Seminary, Fort Worth, TX

Rev. C. D. Fisher - Followers of Christ Baptist Church

Dr. G. L. Ford, Jr. - Rose Hill Missionary Baptist Church, Pine Bluff

Rev. J. Ford - Neighborhood Missionary Baptist Church

Rev. K. G. Free - Greater Mt. Carmel Baptist Church

Rev. J. C. Fulkerson - Truevine Independent Baptist Church

Special Thanks

Rev. L. Gee - McKinley Avenue Baptist Church
Rev. J. C. Gilkey - Timothy Baptist Church
Rev. L. Gillespie - Street Ministry Inc., OKC
Rev. D. L. Gordon - Calvary Baptist Church
Dr. B. Graham - Worldwide Evangelist
Rev. H. S. Green Sr. - Greater Holy Divine Baptist Church
Evangelist O. B. Green - The Gospel Hour Broadcast
Rev. D. Hardy - Eastland Baptist Church, Tulsa, OK
Dr. B. Harrison - Southwest Baptist Church
Rev. D. Hart - Glovers Grove Missionary Baptist Church, Walls, MS
Rev. H. Higgins - Madison Street C.O.G.I.C.
Overseer E. Hill - Church of the Living God P.G.O.T.
Dr. E. H. Hill - Mt. Horeb Baptist Church
Rev. K. Hobbs - Street Ministry Inc., OKC
Rev. M. Howard Jr. - Greater Marshall Memorial Baptist Church
Rev. T. H. Hubbard - Greater Shiloh Baptist Church
Rev. H. Hunter - Pleasant Ridge Baptist Church
Rev. C. Hunter - Mt. Calvary Baptist Church, Wellston, OK
Rev. W. Island Jr. - Progressive National Baptist Convention
Rev. R.T. Jackson - First Baptist Church, Kingfisher, OK
Dr. W.K.Jackson - St. John Missionary Baptist Church
Rev. L. Jacobs - Jesus First Baptist Church, Stroud, OK
Rev. W.C. Jacobs - 56th Street Christian Center, Tulsa, OK
Rev. G. James - Oklahoma City Councilman
Bishop L. Johnson - Church of the Living P.G.O.T.
Rev. A. Johnson - New Hope Baptist Church, Galveston, TX
Rev. H. Joseph - Salem Baptist Church, Jones, OK
Rev. B. T. Killens - Evening Chapel Baptist Church

Special Thanks

Rev. R. Kinnard - New Hope Baptist Church, Langston, OK
Rev. L. Kirk - The Loving St. James Baptist Church
Rev. M. Liggins - Christian Temple Baptist Church
Rev. W. Loggins - Friendship Baptist Church
Elder A. Long - Church of the Living God P.G.O.T.
Rev. B. Lovejoy - Southern Baptist Church Home Missions
Rev. A.B. Martin - St. Matthews Baptist Church, Eagletown, OK
Dr. E. Mayes - Unity Baptist Church
Rev. L. Mays - First Baptist Church, Luther, OK / "Whatever You Need, God Has It Ministry"
Rev. R. Mays - Mt. Carmel Baptist Church
Rev. J.L. Mayshack, Sr. - Tabernacle Baptist Church
Rev. V.H. McCowen - Union Baptist Church
Dr. G.C. McCutchen - Mt. Zion Baptist Church, Tulsa, OK
Dr. J.V. McGee - Through the Bible Radio Broadcast
Rev. C. Muse - St. James Baptist Church
Rev. J. Moore - Christian Life Missionary Baptist Church
Rev. S. Moore - Harrison Baptist Church
Prof. H. Morris - Southwestern Baptist Theological Seminary,Fort Worth, TX
Rev. D.W. Nash - Mt. Horeb Baptist Church, Bristow, OK
Rev. E.R. Neal - Mt. Olive Baptist Church
Rev. L. Nealy - Mt. Moriah Baptist Church
Rev. L. Parker - St. James Baptist Church
Dr. W.B. Parker - The Loving St. James Baptist Church
Bishop F. Patton - Church of the Living God P.G.O.T.
Deacon L. Patton - Church of the Living God P.G.O.T.
Rev. L. Pendarvis - Street Ministry Inc.
Dr. A. Phillips - Mt. Gilead Baptist Church, Denver, CO
Bishop A. Ponder - Church of the Living God C.W.F.F.

Special Thanks

Rev. W. Preston - Mt. Lebanon Baptist Church

Rev. H. Prince - Mt. Triumph A.M.E. Church

Rev. J.D. Provo - New Hope Baptist Church

Rev. L.B. Quinn - Sherman Chapel A.M.E. Church

Rev. R. Redic - Wildewood Baptist Church

Dr. J.A. Reed - Fairview Baptist Church

Dr. P. Reeder - Congress of Christian Education, Progressive

Dr. O. Roberts - World Renowned Evangelist

Dr. T.J. Roberts - Evangelistic Baptist Church

Rev. J. Roby - Baptist Temple, Norman, OK

Dr. D. Roland - St. Luke Baptist Church

Dr. F.D. Roseborough - Paradise Baptist Church

Overseer W.J. Sherman - Church of the Living God P.G.O.T.

Dr. M.L. Shepard - President of Progressive National Baptist Convention, Inc.

Rev. R. Simmons - First Baptist Church, Seminole, OK

Rev. B. Smith - Emmanuel Baptist Church

Rev. J. A. Smith - Greater Mt. Carmel Baptist Church

Rev. K. Smith - St. John Missionary Baptist Church

Rev. L. Smith - St. John Baptist Church, Ponca City, OK

Rev. G.S. Smith - Wildewood Baptist Church

Rev. G. Spriggs - Second Baptist Church, Prague, OK

Dr. S. Tatum - Professor of Preaching, Southwestern Theological Seminary, Fort Worth, TX

Rev. J. Temple - Trinity Baptist Church

Rev. J. Thigpyn - Paradise Baptist Church

Rev. J. Thompson - St. James Baptist Church

Dr. O. Thompson - Professor of Evangelism, Southwestern Theological Seminary, Fort Worth, TX

Rev. A.R. Threatt, III - Emmanuel Baptist Church, Boley, Ok

Special Thanks

Rev. A.W. Tubbs - Mt. Olive Baptist Church, McCloud, OK

Rev. J. Tucker - New Zion Baptist Church

Rev. M.L. Tucker - Pilgrim Rest Baptist Church

Dr. C. Vaughan - Southwestern Baptist Theological Seminary, Professor, Fort Worth, TX

Rev. H.A. Walker - Truevine Independent Baptist Church

Rev. L. Walker Sr. - Rayfield Baptist Church, Muskogee, OK

Rev. H. Wallace - Greater Mt. Rose Baptist Church

Rev. R.L. Wandick - First Baptist Church, Green Pastures

Rev. W.A. Webb - St. Andrews Baptist Church, Tulsa, OK

Rev. J.L. Wesley - Metropolitan Baptist Church, Las Vegas, NV

Dr. F. White - Mt. Sinai Missionary Baptist, Kansas City, MO

Rev. J.W. Whittington - Mt. Nebo Baptist Church, Omaha, NE

Rev. F.L. Wilson - Truevine Baptist Church and Missions

Dr. B. Williams - New Jerusalem Church of God in Christ

Rev. G. Woodberry - Mt. Olive Baptist Church

Rev. W.B. Woodberry - First Baptist Church, Hicks Addition

Rev. C. Woody - Garden Addition Baptist Church

Rev. J. Woodfork - Community Baptist Church, Norman, OK

Rev. C.D. Wyatt - Paradise Baptist Church

All Professors at Southwestern Baptist Theological Seminary, Fort Worth, TX

All Pastors involved in the Northeast Project

All Pastors involved in the Progressive Baptist Convention

All Pastors involved in the Oklahoma Baptist State Convention

All Pastors involved in the Simultaneous Revival, OKC, OK

All Pastors involved in the Ministerial Alliance, Muskogee, OK

All Pastors involved in the Ministerial Alliance, OKC,OK

All Pastors involved in the C.C.S.R.

Bro. G. Kimmell - An "ontime" supporter of Street Ministry Inc.

Special Thanks

Aunt Johnnie Jacobs

Aunt Hortense Jackson and Aunt Laverne Madison

All Aunts, Uncles, Cousins and Other Relatives

Aunt "B" , Beulah Ponder, especially for helping my son

Grandma Leona Jacobs

Grandpa Tom and Rilla Madison

Elder E. and Wife Martha Hill - Neighbors who helped me tremendously growing up

Mr. Sherman Menser - A brother and a Soul Winner

Mr. and Mrs. Roosevelt Moore, Christian supporters, Galveston, TX
The Daily Oklahoman Newspaper, KTOK 1000, and FM 91
Rev. Marvin L. Smith - Publisher, Campbell Road Press
Mr. Russell Perry - Black Chronicle Newspaper
Irene Jenkins - Mother-in-law, a great source of encouragement
Mother Reed of St. James Baptist Church

Mother Willie Wilson - The First Mother of the Christian Life

Mrs. Johnnie Dickerson - My first Sunday School Teacher

Mother Jackson - Church of the Living God P.G.O.T. - VBS Teacher
Mr. Ben Tipton - Former OKC Councilman and D.J.
Mr & Mrs. Pleas Williams - Our community store owners.
Mrs. Jimmie Neece - A dear friend and beautician for my wife

Mr. Fred & Mrs. Nancy Davis - Great encouragers

Mrs. Bobbie Taylor - Director of Guthrie Job Corp.

Mr. Howard Williams - Owner/Manager of KTLV Radio Station

Bro. Carl Jones and The St. James Men's Chorus

KOCO-TV 5, KFOR-TV 4, KOCB-TV-34, KOKH-TV 25, Channel 14

Bill my Boss at the Chicken Farm, Jones,Ok

Larry Jones and Feed The Children

KWTV Channel 9 News - Staff
Bro Taft Jordan - Fellow worker

Don Rogers - President of Spencer State Bank and Friend

Billy Brown - Schoolmate, Friend

My Sons in the Gospel

Minister Frank McClarty
Minister Kenneth Adams
Minister Mickael Stephens
Minister Ron Simms
Minister Gregory Benjamin
Minister Ron Scott
Minister Michael Washington
Minister James Alston
Minister James Moss
Minister Wayne Lee
Minister Eddie Gill
Minister Ray Brown
Minister Ralph Boyattia
Minister Isaiah Sierson
Minister Curtis Liggins
Minister Titus Jacobs
Minister Bruce Jarman

Other Ministers Associated with Christian Life

Pastor Terry Wilson
Pastor Wallace Youngblood
Dr. Cliet Wilburn
Rev. Robert Haynes
Pastor Tony Wise
Rev. Jeffery Cook
Pastor Carl Douglas
Rev. Todd Coleman
Pastor Henry Gunn
Pastor Walter Jacobs
Rev. Claude Carruthers
Rev. John DuBose

Trustees Past and Present

Ron Sims, Eddie Gill, William Clark, Frank McClarty, Steve Young, Ralph Boyattia, Shirley Nero, Patsy Nolen, Lois Pollard, William Dockery, Thomas Gipson, Michael Washington, Michael Jackson, Walter Jacobs, James Alston, Freddie Qualls, and Albert Lee

Deacons Past and Present

Albert Lee, Frank McClarty, Steve Young, Dennis Pearson, William Clark, Brian Collier, and Richie Guess

Pastor Jacobs, a spokesman for the community.

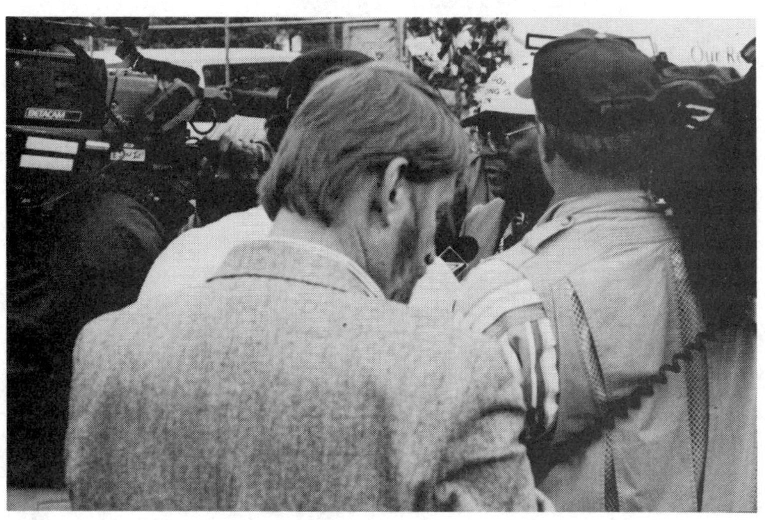

Above and Below: Pastor Jacobs during Church Services in the sanctuary of the Christian Life Missionary Baptist Church.

About The Author

Dr. Jayel Jacobs, Jr., received a Bachelor of Arts Degree in Sociology from Central State College, a Masters of Religious Education Degree from Southwestern Theological Seminary in Ft. Worth, Texas, and a Doctorate of Ministry Degree from Central America University, Ministries, Inc. in Kansas City, Kansas. He is the former Director of the Street Ministry Inc., where he and others preached on the streets, and saw thousands come to the Lord Jesus Christ across America.

He is the former Moderator and President of a state convention. He taught Evangelism at the National Baptist Convention Inc. and the Progressive National Baptist Convention Inc. Dr. Jacobs is a radio and television personality who has supported God's work and God's people around the world.

He has served the Lord both as an Evangelist and a Pastor. He was one of the first full-time black Evangelists in America, for over four years. He Pastors the Christian Life Missionary Baptist Church of Oklahoma City, Oklahoma, which he helped to organize beginning with three members, seventeen years ago. Christian Life, an evangelistic church on the move, has as one of its goals to meet human needs because God cares. Various extensions have been established by Dr. Jacobs throughout the United States and have become self-supporting churches.

Pastor Jacobs has been preaching for over 27 years and has the vision to compassionately communicate the good news of Jesus Christ with lost people, that they may be led to believe on Him as Savior, and follow Him as Lord. His desire is not only to lead people to Christ, but to see them mature and become victorious Christians.

Written straight from the heart, "From Preaching on the Streets, To Pastoring in the Pulpit" - With an Emphasis on Evangelism, Dr. Jacobs shares his life's story, which depicts his methods of evangelism. If you long to do the work of the Lord, then this immensely practical book is God's answer for you.

A display of Grace, to God be all of the Glory!

TO ORDER
THIS PUBLICATION
AND

"God's Gift, Your Blessing"
A Pastor's Aide Guide
and
Others

WRITE OR CALL:
Christian Life Missionary Baptist Church
4621 NE 23rd
Oklahoma City, Ok 73121

Books / Video / Audio Productions
(405) 424-4041 / 1-800-429-4621

Personal Checks, Money Orders,
Mastercard, Visa, Discover Card, or
American Express Accepted

Allow 4-6 weeks for Delivery

Out in the community making a difference to the Glory of God and Salvation of Mankind.

Food sack giveaways at a 300 Foot-Soldier Prayer, Praise, and Pep Rally where over 2,000 were contacted, more than 200 accepted Christ, and 32 were actually baptized that night at the Rally sponsored by the Northeast Project.

Morning Worship Service.

Oklahoma City Public Schools involved in the March Against Crime

A crowd at the Parade Against Crime in Northeast Oklahoma City along with Christian Life members seizing the opportunity to share Christ.

Preaching alone in an apartment complex in Shreveport, Louisiana.

TO MY CHILDREN
Deya, Jayel III, & Joseph

Thank you for giving up the times

that might have seemed lost.

Thank you for giving in

and allowing me to minister the Word of God

with freedom to others. Thank you for

carrying on in my absence.

I am truly thankful for you.

You have been blessed and you are a blessing.

Your Father,

In Love

An aerial view of the Christian Life Missionary Baptist Church and Properties Oklahoma City, Oklahoma.

There are some tremendous benefits for Evangelizing!

"The fruit of the righteous is a tree of life; and he that winneth souls is wise." - Proverbs 11:30

"And Jesus answered and said, Verily I say unto you, There is no man that hath left house, or brethren, or sisters, or father, or mother, or wife, or children, or lands, for my sake, and the gospel's, But he shall receive an hundredfold now in this time, houses, and brethren, and sisters, and mothers, and children, and lands, with persecutions; and in the world to come eternal life. - Mark 10:29-30

"And they that be wise shall shine as the brightness of the firmament; and they that turn many to righteousness as the stars for ever and ever." - Daniel 12:3